Oct. 2007
To: Mark

Enjoy! A bit of a
"Red herring" but I
needed to write it.
Nice mtg. you (IAD to LAX).
(Page 80 was 1st chapter
written).

A true 1st edition
M. D. Stuart
(aka Marilyn McClain)

R I T C H

By M.D. Stuart

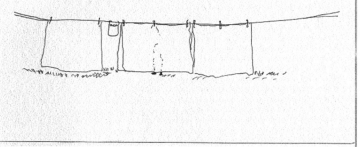

M.D. Under the Sheets

Stories and Journals for

"Ritch" Living Without Perfection

International Standard Book Number 0-87012-671-7
Library of Congress Control Number 2001119429
Printed in the United States of America
Copyright © 2001 by M.D. Stuart
Fairfax, VA
All Rights Reserved
2001

McClain Printing Company
Parsons, WV 26287
www.mcclainprinting.com

Dedication

This compilation from my journals and recollections is dedicated to all creatures that feel that they don't quite measure up to, nor accept, the world's definition of beauty.

To each and every kind person that has come into my life, I give you this book with immeasurable gratitude and love. Thank you for your kindness that soothed my aching heart.

To those that hurt me, you helped make me stronger.

...and to Jim, my husband ...we'll just have to talk later.

Acknowledgements

For encouragement and affirmation: My very own children, Peter and Sarah, and my late husband, Jim.

For encouragement and reading: Bob, Brett, Dad, Dianne, Jackie, Janis, Jessica, Israel, Linda, Michael, Nancy, Rick, Rik, Roger, Tim and the 6th grade Sunday school classes at my church.

For encouragement and help: All of the above and the Spirit that moves…

Foreword

Since history and art were first recorded, the emphasis on physical wholeness and beauty has been exalted by societies around the world. The continuance of humanity hinges on the attraction of symmetry in facial and physical appearance. Physical health and robustness also strongly influence our ability to catch and keep a mate long enough to continue our species.

When a baby is in-utero, or just born, doctors and parents anxiously evaluate overall appearance, such as counting fingers and toes, as well as viability of the baby, heart, lungs, etc. The happy parent sighs with relief when observing their baby after birth: the nicely shaped head, existence of all body parts, and everything seems in working order. When something is awry with the baby, the parents are devastated. They might weep, wring their hands and seek consolation for this "tragedy" befallen them. Some parents give up the child to a home if the handicap is too severe. A heart murmur or problem *inside* the baby will be difficult for the parents when not life threatening. However, there is a deeper emotional reaction by the family if the baby is missing an arm, leg, has a disfigured face, or other visible imperfections on the *outside* of the baby.

Most parents know that an imperfect child is not well accepted in society. So plans are made to have the imperfection minimized or corrected. The parents will consider the child's future and general well being, of course, but will need to deal with their own anxiety. Often, their anxiety leads to attempts to cover up what can't be made to "go away". Just like throwing a large brass blanket over the statue of Franklin D. Roosevelt's legs and wheelchair, a way must be found to cover it up. Cover it all up. This need to correct, cover up, or hide, the imperfection is proof that neither the person, nor the public, can handle the shame.

Reality: the imperfect person, child and adult, will be visible to the critical eyes and mouth of the world. The people behind the eyes won't understand the enraging impact of how, where and how long they look at the societal "leper". The people behind the mouths that ask too many questions won't understand how questions are like bells clanging for all to hear - the shame that is felt. They won't understand the impact because I, and others like me, won't tell them.

In recent news, we are hearing about sperm and egg sales via the internet to create the perfect baby that will be intelligent and beautiful. It is pretty much guaranteed by the genetic match. Cloning such a person will probably become a viable option in this century. This book doesn't address the morality, ethics, or religion on this topic. The book may, in fact, for some readers, support the need to avoid creating the imperfect baby, and that any price is worth it. Even if science can eliminate the imperfect baby, injury from traffic accidents or war will continue. Therefore, the emotional challenges of being physically imperfect will continue.

This book may help enlighten people by describing the emotional impact on the flawed one, engendered from a negative reaction from society. In spite of this, even *because* of this, humor and joy can exist in great abundance.

By airing my struggles and triumphs publicly, it is hoped that people might become more aware of the impact of the simple, elongated stare, whispered remark, or overly direct question, and the difficulties unique to each imperfection. I also hope that other people-of-difference will publish their own stories. Only through public expression of our hidden thoughts can people begin to understand the hurt and struggles. If we are silent, we are enabling the societal behavior to continue, unchecked and unchanged.

There is a great "ritchness" of life when a person is met with the unique emotional challenge of being different. That challenge alone is enough without adding the cruelty of others.

This book represents what I believe is a sample message from millions of persons in the world: the victims of difference, who feel they must suffer in silence.

~~~

I grew up in Falls Church, Virginia, in the 1950s in a normanrockwellian setting. I was born with a congenital birth defect of the left fibula, a clubfoot. My left leg is five inches shorter than my right leg. This book describes my experiences and feelings about life growing up different in a society that values external appearances. Even though I have been a relatively successful professional, wife and mother, feelings of shame and unacceptance continued past childhood, becoming especially acute after my second husband died.

The chapters alternate between childhood and adulthood to establish relevancy, growth and an acute appreciation of life as a direct result of both painful and joyful experiences. Many of the drawings and text are from childhood diaries and adult journals over a forty-five-year period.

I am hopeful this book is cathartic to other persons who are imperfect, physically challenged or otherwise "different" than the majority. It may also help sensitize the "normal" reader to the emotional struggles of being different. I think everyone will be able to relate just a little.

My life has been truly fabulous, incredible, challenging and chock-a-block with happiness and tragedies so far. I hope you find the book helpful, sometimes humorous, and very hopeful.

Kidney Garden

1956

The upstairs of my house was a whole separate world. It is the first world I can remember in my frontal lobe of consciousness. My earliest memories occurred in that very small space in my straight-up-and-down house.

I have lived here since I was two. My sister and I share a bedroom with a sagging double bed with a silk down comforter, and striped flat feather pillows. Our room has two windows and a little alcove with a slanted desk. My mama says it is antique and warped. The bathroom is across the hall and has little black and white tiles and a window over the john. The john is funny because it talks! I do not know what cussing is, but my Mama says that's what my Daddy does when the john won't shut up after flushing. "Will someone *please* get up and jiggle the *%$# john?!"

One of my favorite things to do is play in the sink in the bathroom. I take Ivory soap and rub it across the three openings under the faucets while the water is running. It makes really pretty rainbow bubbles over the holes.

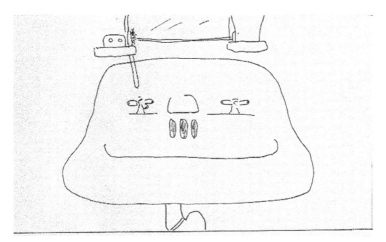

Sometimes a slat that supports the bed falls down; we lean or fall depending on which side falls. During very, very hot summer nights the only way to get to sleep is to fight for the side of the bed against the plaster wall. It is always cool. You just press your body flat against it to feel better for a while.

I got my very own room a little while ago. It is very tiny. I used to fall out of bed a lot so Mama would put a chair backwards against the side of the bed but that wouldn't always help. She says I have goose eggs on my head. I do better now.

I like where we put my bed and dresser, but when I lay in bed all I can see is the three doors. One goes to the hall - the bathroom is at the other end - and one has a little ladder in it to the attic with the bats. The center door is my mama's closet. It is always closed.

My room has two windows. The one by the door to the attic opens onto a small ledge at the side of the house. The other window faces the front of the house. Right after Thanksgiving they light the Christmas star on top of the blue water tower next to the State Theatre. I can only see the side of the star, so it's just a straight line. But I know when it is lit that's the time to get real excited about Christmas!

I have lots of fun in here with my dolls. I pretend a lot in here, too. It is fun. A couple of weeks ago I had to go to the hospital. After I got home, for three nights I remember seeing little scary men running out from under my bed. They made small shadows in the glow of the little brown nightlight Mama put in here. Mama says it must have been the medicine they gave me, a painkiller or something. I was very scared of those little things running around on my floor. One night I called for Mama real loud to come get them away but my voice made no noise!

My mama helps me get dressed every day. I can do a lot of it myself but I still have trouble tying the bows on the back of my dresses. My arms just won't reach and anyway I'm still learning to tie my shoes. Mama puts the brace on for me and ties it. I can't wait to do this stuff for myself!

My room is my whole wide world. Sometimes I am lonely here. Sometimes I cry when I go to sleep when I feel like nobody likes me.

I like it when my cousin Laurel comes over to play. She does scary things sometimes. She will open the window and climb out on that ledge.

My Room
(Hall, Mama's closet, way to attic)
118 N. Fairfax St. Falls Church

When Mama catches her, she tells Laurel she could fall and kill herself!

One day Mama says I need to start Kidney Garden. I don't want to go but she says it will be nice because it will be in Mrs. White's house. The first day I am terrified because I have to get into a big fat black car that has a square black board sign nailed on top that says "Mrs. White's School". Mrs. White is driving it, too. I want to stay at home and play. I don't want to get in that car. But Mama makes me get in it.

When I go in her house through the side door I can see some other kids. I like to put my coat on a hook I can reach. Scary, scary thing. Mrs. White has a big cage on a big table in a big room. And guess what is in the cage? Squirrels. Lots of 'em. The one boy I like is named George but I feel kind of funny the way he and the other children look at me.

We color and play which I like okay. But my favorite thing is snack. First Mrs. White tells us to line up single file, which means we all look straight ahead behind each other. Then she tells us to go quietly up the steps to her attic. My brace doesn't fit very well on each stair and I don't like people behind me looking at it. When we get to the top of the stairs I can see a table that has some graham crackers and milk. I *love* this part at Mrs. White's. I eat it too fast and have to wait for everyone else before we go back downstairs.

It rained real hard on the first day and my mama came to get me with an umbrella.

I missed a bunch of kidney garden when I had to go to the hospital

again for an operation on my leg. I told my mama that if I went in to the hospital I would miss my turn leading the Pledge of Allegiance. I didn't know what they were going to do to me in the hospital. I was very, very scared of the operation, and I was mad, too. When it was over, my leg was in a cast. The last day of kidney garden my Daddy and Mama drove me to Mrs. White's and someone brought over a red wagon, put me in it and rolled me over the grass to her big flagpole in the back yard. I could see all the children and their parents were there as I was being pulled along in the wagon. I was embarrassed. Then I was surprised to know that I would lead the Pledge of Allegiance right there from my wagon. That was a hard thing to do sitting down.

Senior Prom

1969

Mama and Daddy went to North Carolina to play golf on the weekend of the senior prom. I haven't been to a prom before. I asked Robbie if he would take me as he was home from college for the summer. He is a very good friend. I had a crush on him some years back but have settled down after having a crush on all my guy friends. He accepted the invite. I bought a full-length cotton ribbed yellow simple dress, straight a-line with a low back. It was very plain but elegant. I stupidly had my hair done and looked like a whore. Good thing my folks were away. I felt very grown-up preparing myself alone in my folks' bedroom. We would go with two other couples in one of their father's Cadillac. We were going to dinner somewhere in upper Georgetown and then to a party at a friend's house nearby. Robbie called to ask me the color of my dress. I knew he was asking so that he could order flowers or have his mother do the deed. It felt very strange to have a date for this event. I felt ashamed accepting flowers and worried if he was just being "nice" so I'd have a chance to go to the "last" prom. I chose not to think about it too much. Robbie is a very fun guy.

Robbie showed up at my front door holding a white box, looking wonderfully ridiculous. He had taped fake sideburns on his face, wore his Dad's long tail tux jacket, a light blue cummerbund, a bow tie, blue jeans and tennis shoes. We looked like complete opposites. This is the sixties so anything goes. I loved it. (Once Robbie shaved his head and wore a beret with his good citizen's medal pinned on it. Robbie was deliciously different, weird in fact. He played an electric bass guitar and sang "Gloria" bouncing up and down at his knees.)

Amputation
(I don't *think* so!)

1964

When Mama and Daddy said they had made an appointment in Washington and Boston for me "to see doctors to explore the possibility of a Symes amputation," I recall thinking that I *really* needed to be brave for this one. My parents seemed especially concerned about my appearance as I was just entering adolescence. They were very smart to consider my best interests, my psyche. I guess they pictured me sitting home alone for my entire high school years. They probably also feared that I might never get married and leave home.

I went along with the humiliating appointment at Children's Hospital in Boston. They x-rayed every part of me and did not respect my privacy, my dignity. I was told the front of the foot would have to be amputated so that I could wear a prostheses. "It will really look natural," they said. They said I would heal over the summer, learn to walk with it and probably miss half a year of school. But wasn't it worth it? I wanted very badly to please my folks and to show the world how brave I was, so I made the appointment at Sibley Hospital myself.

A month before the scheduled surgery, my mother took me to a very old building in Alexandria where they would show me the prostheses, the lower left leg and foot that would feel "lifelike". I waited in a small room. The place looked like an old factory with high ceilings and there were prosthetic limbs of every size hanging like cow parts in a butcher shop. "I am okay. I am okay," I said to myself. Then, they brought me the leg.

I was so horrified I could barely speak. It felt cold and was hard plastic with straps at the top that would hook above my knee. The color was the color of the legs of my barbie doll, not lily white like mine. I really had to work hard at pushing down the emotions. I felt more horror than disappointment. Riding silently in the car next to mother, I let the tears roll out of my eyes but didn't let her see them. The next day I called the minister of my church and made an appointment to see him. The day I spoke with him, I concluded that maybe I was born this way for a reason. Maybe part of my purpose in life was to go on just as I am...no amputation and obviously deformed.

I think my parents were disappointed when I told them my decision. I felt like a coward.

Over the years the decision proved to be the right one for me because my orthopedic surgeon said I would never have walked as well with the prosthetic limb, and my life was to be "ritcher" than I could ever imagine...

A Saturday

1959

Spring, a warm Saturday morning about 11 o'clock in the morning. A square-legged curly hair girl of eight years is galloping down our 18 wooden steps to eat breakfast before a hard day of play at making mudpies and climbing trees. She's Laurel, my father's sister's youngest child and my cousin.

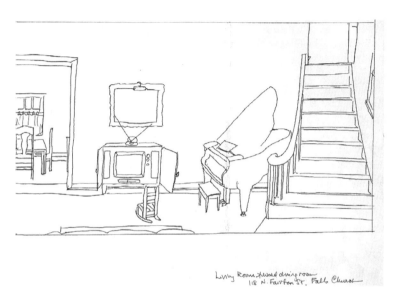

Living Room toward dining room
118 N. Fairfax St. Falls Church

I'm trying to clomp down the steps after her as loudly but I nearly trip since Mama waxed the steps yesterday. I slow down cautiously thinking I can only jump the last two steps, not six like my cousin. I'll work on three tomorrow. The trouble is I always lock my knees when I land, but I've been working on that.

We arrive at the table where my Daddy sits grimacing, turning red. Laurel says, as ever, "Sorry, Uncle Fred. I keep forgetting…about the steps." He shakes his head and frowns. Despite the noise she makes, I think he still loves her. Exit Daddy for a game of golf.

After finishing a bowl of good ol' wholesome cornflakes, one of my Mama's best dishes, Laurel washes down her repast with a fingernail from her index finger and little finger of her left hand. "Laurel," my mother asks, "Hasn't your mother broken you of that awful habit yet? What happened to that gunk she put on your fingers to get you to stop?" Laurel giggles and says that she likes the stuff.

Here comes Nancy, my only sister, clad in her pointed red flats, circle skirt, peter pan blouse and her straight red plastic barrettes holding back her black, "mama chopped" hair. I'm gonna steal those barrettes soon, though I've passed my stealing stage. Mama only gets me blue or pink barrettes for *my* "mama chopped" hair. Over her face are used-to-be-pink, now yellow-with-age plastic glasses just like mine. Actually the only difference is our above-the-knee appearance. She's taller, thinner, and four years older. I'm wearing her hand-me-downs. The only time we get new clothes is at Christmas, and they always match.

Anyway...Mama and Nancy leave in our coral '57 Pontiac, rattling and throwing gravel from our driveway. We'd behave all right, Laurel and I, just like eight year olds.

After swinging ourselves sick on the swings in back of my house, we decide it's time for lunch. Mama is back and washing breakfast dishes. We plead for our favorite lunch: peanut butter and butter sandwiches. Mama's never tasted as good as my Aunt's (Aunt Sarah, Laurel's mom) though. You can really mess it up if you don't use Peter Pan peanut butter and real butter, not margarine, and gotta use Brick Oven bread. Any other is second rate. Mama's are second rate. Today she is out of margarine (we never have butter). We have peanut butter and honey, which is pretty good and we take our sandwiches out to the swings, two rectangular pieces of sandwich in each grubby little hand (Aunt Sarah's are always cut in four pieces, party style).

There we are, rubbing our toes (Laurel's toes, my shoes) in the dirt under the swings discussing what we are going to do next: ride our bikes to the five and dime store or make mudpies, when Laurel begins to whine. I look over and tears are running down her fat little cheeks. A yellow jacket is about to enter her mouth in great pursuit of her honey and peanut butter! I don't know whether to laugh or scream for Mama. By the time I get my hollers to reach Mama's-always-deaf-to-a-crisis ears, Laurel has gotten her mouth closed without the bee entering. She has moved two hundred feet away.

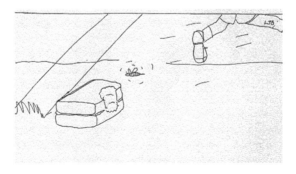

Laurel lets the tears dry (she never wipes her eyes) and we're off to the tree up against the side of my house where the shade and dampness are just right for mudpies. The pot pie tin pans and our best digging and smoothing sticks are still there from the last time and we get right down to business. The big decision is whether we want to make vanilla mudpies (with dry dirt), with chocolate icing (wet dirt on top), or grass pies (wet and dry mixed with lovely grass bits on top). We decide to make them all. They always look good enough to eat. After completing this task we dump the stuff back on the ground and stomp it down, since it would be cheating to reuse these next time. We go into the house to wash the dirt off of our cold, mud-dried hands. Laurel always gets cleaner than I do somehow, probably because she doesn't have to worry about dirt under her fingernails.

We still have plenty of daytime left, so I plead to Daddy for money. I find him sitting in his chair in the living room, sweating and smelly from losing his golf game. He visibly shrinks when he hears us coming, Laurel *slamming* the metal door behind us. He's about to say something, I think because he's sitting bolt upright in the chair. But I am on him so fast with hand held out that he doesn't get a chance. Too tired to argue and wanting to get rid of us in a hurry, he groans as he leans forward for his wallet and gives me a dollar bill. Mama always gives me fifteen cents or a quarter, but Daddy is a pushover. Laurel gets an allowance every week, but I'm sure I pocket two hundred dollars more a year merely by using my direct, though persuasive, manner and big doey eyes. It's probably not the doeyness as much as the way my eyes cross that gets him. That expensive eye operation last year was a pitiful waste of money.

We're off. Behind us I hear a great sigh from Daddy.

Living Room 118 N. Fairfax St., Fall Chead

The bike ride to Robertson's Five and Dime is always exhilarating. We feel such freedom as we pedal past pedestrians on the sidewalk down Broad

Street...Laurel on her twenty-six inch boy's speed bike and me following faithfully behind on my twenty inch pink bike with training wheels. There is a deserted lot off the way, and we decide to pedal through it. A little of the country in that weed-ridden lot, I think, as we pedal past dandelions and ragweed. Suddenly, as my right leg comes up from a down pedal, I'm wracked by pain. I whine and scream, "Laurel, *Stop*!!!". I shake three smashed yellow jackets out of my pink and white checked shorts. Nancy's shorts are so baggy that those little fiends couldn't help but get caught. My first bee stings, and I'm frantic. Laurel says it's okay, so I dry my tears on my red and yellow striped T-shirt and we continue our trek.

We enter Robertson's. Laurel flies to the candy counter up front and works madly filling up bags with wax red lips, tiny juice filled wax bottles and red hots, which I hate. I go over to my favorite counter, wallets and purses. They all usually cost about a dollar so I debate as to whether I should get one or buy candy. I decide to purchase a red purse with little compartments since it has already been a week since I bought a wallet or purse. It's a real bargain at eighty-nine cents, so I go back to the candy counter where Laurel is still filling up bags. I pick up a box of jujubes. We go to the cashier who is waiting, smiling. She has taken a killing every time we come in. Mr. Robertson has cleverly kept that nickel-junk-toys-in-a-plastic-capsule machine by the exit door, and we can't resist trying our luck to get what we see through the glass. But all the good stuff's on top. We talk about what we hope we get and place our nickels in the slot. I get a tiny black spider and Laurel gets a little fan. We trade of course. As ever, I can't get the thing open so Laurel, with her brute strength, cracks them both open with her teeth.

We gleefully hop onto our bikes, Laurel wearing her wax red lips and holding her bag of other healthful goodies over the handlebar. I pull my new purse and jujubes out of my bag and put the jujubes in the purse, the purse over the handlebar and the bag on my book holder in back.

Off we go and soon we are coasting down the hill on Fairfax Street with the wind in our hair and into my driveway. Laurel throws down her bike and I put down my kickstand. We're back in the house to the delight of my parents.

Laurel has to be home by dinnertime so we decide that we better do something that is short and fun. We decide to torture Penny, my dog, in the basement. If anyone made that cocker spaniel mean, Laurel and I did. To go about having this fun, we place old dining room chairs at certain places on the red and black tiled floor. We call Penny and taunt her with "Get the spider, Penny!" which makes her insanely chase after us. The object is to run from chair to chair without getting bitten, stepping only on the red tiles. I poop out after the second chair. Soon Laurel is crying because Penny is growling and nipping at her ferociously. Mama is fed up and yells at us to stop it. I think Daddy has bitten his tongue while trying to peacefully read *Reader's Digest*. With time still left we begin a friendly game of cards. "War" is always fun using four decks. Halfway through the pile we begin to bicker at each other. Mama enters, says it's time for Laurel to go home and, "How many times do I have to tell you not to use my good bridge cards?"

We slowly tread up the stairs to pack Laurel's overnight paper bag and soon we part mournfully as though we'll never see each other again. "See you in church tomorrow," she said."

"Okay, I'll meet you in the bathroom at 11:30," I reply. Church starts at 11:15.

Generally, dinner in my family is great fun for all of us. Mama feels that it is very important since it is the only time we're all together. I'm always the first one at the table. Nancy knows better. As the first person downstairs I have to set the table, a droll, unhappy chore. I always do it. "Can't Nancy do it sometimes?" I ask Mama. Mama says she has to study. Great excuse. She's just hiding. I also serve as butler to announce when dinner is served.

I'm *sooooo* hungry and we can't start until we're all together and the grace is said. My turn tonight (I hate it!). I'm usually hungrier because the lunch Mama packs for me is one sandwich, one apple, three butter cookies you can stick your finger through and three cents for milk. I eat the sandwich and cookies, hate the fruit and save the three cents for an ice cream at the end of the week.

It usually takes six separate calls to get them to dinner. It really irritates them. I get the blame for Mama's dirty work. My father and sister finally come to the table, but I have already eaten my chunk of lettuce (the salad) and drank part of my chocolate milk. I mutter grace of, "Thanks a lot for this food and may it help build our bodies in twelve different ways and fit us for the duties we perform or are about to or...AMEN!" This food, that has hopefully been blessed, is usually a chunk or ball of meat covered in a lot of catsup to hide it. Mama says you have to have a vegetable so we always get green or yellow wax beans. So bland are my mother's dishes that my father risks a heart attack by snowing a blanket of salt onto his food. Nancy and Daddy love baked potatoes. I hate 'em, so we have baked potatoes with every meal. Dad uses a half stick of cold margarine on his and Nancy devours the whole thing muttering praises to Mama, "You know how I love baked potatoes!" Mama smiles and I saw away the burnt skin and take two screwed up mouthfuls of the white meat.

A footnote about Mama: My mother was a Brownie leader, which must have been a terrible struggle for her...something she felt she had to do or was pushed to do. The first time we met was in our basement where we were tasked to make something ridiculous: some kind of mat to sit on that had stuffing of a Life *or* Post *magazine. These sit-upon things were red and as flat as the magazine! It must be she wanted to do something simple. I'm still not sure what they were. The second time we met was in the backyard. We had a game where you throw peanuts in the shell into an open bag. My mother was from Georgia.*

A Sunday, A Monday

1959

After church - or should I say "bathroom" - the next day, the Stuart's (my family) are invited over to the Brown's (Laurel's family) for lunch. One house is only about a mile from the other. This is a ritual both families enjoy. Laurel and I loved this, of course, because we could be together.

After lunch, we get out Laurel's Barbie dolls and sit on the hard wood floors of the huge foyer of that old Victorian home. Aunt Sarah warns us of a piece of wood splinter sticking up from the floor. We joke about how funny it would be if one us backed onto it and got it in our fanny. Minutes later I'm sliding back for a doll dress and the splinter is very artfully lodged in my bottom. Too embarrassed to call for my aunt, too scared that lockjaw might set in any minute, I run to the bathroom to see if I can dislodge it myself. No luck. So there I was clad in a red face while my aunt removes the three and a half inch long by one quarter inch wide piece of floor and applies the latest thing in no-tears medication, Bactine. Kind of like "ouchless" bandaids and no-nox gasoline. It always stings, ouches and knocks. Too upset and embarrassed to continue playing dolls, my mother takes me home and tells me I will have to see Dr. Weber in the morning. Oh, God, I think. That needle-happy man...a shot for anything and everything and if you don't need one, he gives you one for good measure or good luck or *something!* Anyway, after seeing him there was never a dry eye, a moving arm or a bottom sat upon. He was not exactly gentle in his manner and the lollipops he gave out only meant to me that he wants me to come back tomorrow for another dose of his "medicine". I think that the years that I was seeing him my blood was mostly penicillin, polio vaccine, and booster. Booster didn't do anything but make me ill.

At this comment from my mother, I give the stock question, "Is he going to give me a *shot!?*" And the stock answer, "We'll see," which means yes in all instances. I whine and whine and whine all the rest of the day and evening. My dreams that night include a three hundred-foot hypodermic needle with Dr. Weber at the other end of it cackling.

I wake up, just this once hoping that Mama has forgotten the whole thing and I purposefully get dressed intending to go to school, *not* the doctor. I go to breakfast with my books in hand. Oh, if I can just get out the door, I'll be safe! Mama's sipping her Borden's instant coffee and Dad's going out the door I arrive. "Bye, honey," he says to me. "Virginia, don't forget to pick up my shirts from the cleaners on the way back from Weber's," he says to my mother.

"Oh no, MAMAAAAA!"

"Come on, honey. You didn't forget did you? Belinda (the nurse) got in at 9:00. Isn't that great? She got us in first thing!" I begin to tremble and have that urge to go to sleep, as I always do when about to face a crisis.

I sit all the way there, a thirty-minute ride, in silence punishing my mother for her cruelty. We arrive, go down into the cold basement of his home where his office is located. Arms are becoming sensitized just like meat in a butcher's freezer. All those stupid smiling mothers and babies playing blocks don't know what is about to happen to them. And now my gums are beginning to itch like they do when I'm nervous.

I sit in dead silence only thinking about how it'll feel. It gets worse and worse and worse. Belinda calls my name and we move down the hall. Mama's saying, "He just might not give you a shot."

With new found hope, I give a cheery "Hi!" to Dr. Weber who is waiting for me. He hears about why I am here (the splinter, bottom, etc.) and asks Belinda to prepare a tetanus shot. "Oh, MAMAAAAAA!" I cry. I whine and cling to her arm. Finally, it is done and I can hardly move waiting for the ache to set in. But glad it is over, I take my lollipop and go. Mama tells me to keep moving my arm. I *never* do this and she should know that by now. By the time we get home my arm is so stiff I won't be able to move it for days and I'm very sure to stay ten feet away from everyone so no one bumps into me. I tell everyone to be very careful, sleep on my right side and go through doorways way to the right. After a sandwich Mama says that I should go back to school. But no way. I would if I could make an announcement to the whole school about my arm so that they stay clear. Mama finally concedes.

The next day I'm back in school. Not much to say about school except the way it smells, recess and dumb book reports. I hated recess and would even offer my services to the teacher to help erase the blackboard for half an hour but she would look at my pale, wan little being and usher me out the door with the others. I'm heading out over the blacktop hoping a swing might be free. It takes little energy, it's easy and I hardly ever get one because like today, there's a line waiting for them of other pale, wan, frail little girls. I decide to go where the merry-go-round, jungle gym and slide are located, off the blacktop on a dirt and weeded area. The highest I can get on the jungle gym is one rung but the gym is dangerously crowded today...someone might just dig a heel into my still tender left arm. So, I go to the slide where it is one-at-a-time. Once I get to the top to slide down, I have a *terrible* time trying to get into a sitting position. Left leg over or right, both together is too hard. Somehow I get into a sitting position. Just then the sun comes out directly on to the slide so that the metal is shining, white-hot. I go very slowly since my fat little legs are sticking and pulling as I try to *slide* down. It stings so badly on the back of my legs. Halfway down I stop completely and have to pull myself the rest of the way. After that I frown over to the merry-go-round determined to have fun and recess.

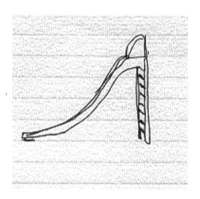

Because of my arm, I make sure I get one whole section to myself as I sit on one of the splinter ridden, brittle boards that connect into a pentagon. As we all start to push with our feet, sideways, and someone else pushes the bar on the outside, I ask myself "Why do I do this?! I *always* get sick on this thing!" It is too late to get off. The ground is spinning by beneath me. The monster kid is pushing faster, laughing villainously. I scream, "Slow down! Stop!" but this makes him go faster and two others come over to help thrill us even more. Now I'm running around the middle trying to PULL the thing to a stop. But my frail, pale, wan little body is trampled beneath the spinning death trap. A good friend runs to my rescue from the slide line and scolds the boys. Dirty and bruised, I climb out of the thing with my glasses hanging lopsided on my fat little face.

I decide there's one last ditch effort: the swings are free and I hobble back to the blacktop to sit on the hot rubber swings. I start to rock my poor self back and forth slowly. As the air begins to cool my face, I decide to go a bit faster.

Three things can happen to me on the swings: pinched fingers or palms from the chains on the swing, trying to stop too suddenly or lose my grip both put me on my knees on the hard blacktop. Today none of these things happen. A not-too-good friend, however, decides to give me a boost. Soon I have visions of being looped all around the top of the swings or landing on the roof of the back of the school in front of me. After more hoarse pleading to stop, the bell rings for the end of recess. I say a prayer of thanks and go in thinking to myself, "I wonder whose idea 'recess' was?"

After school lets out, I begin the trek home around three blocks. (The shortcut is only three hundred yards which I usually use in winter or when I'm real late). Sometimes Laurel and I walk part way together, parting a mailbox on the corner of Cherry Street. We weren't close buddies in school. It all started when, on the third day of first grade, the principal entered the classroom we shared and stated that Laurel was brilliant (smarter than me anyway) and would skip the first grade. She immediately took her place upstairs in Miss Cottini's second grade class. I was so crushed that from then on we had our own separate school buddies but were long lost friends on weekends, holidays, snow days and summers. From then on she would boast to everyone that she was not four months older than me but one third of a whole year! Her and her mathematical mind....

The longer route home is always special. I enjoy the mystery of those houses tucked behind firtrees, bushes and flowers, all dark and cozy. Just as I traverse that stretch of brick sidewalk before I turn on to my street, I think about my hard day of multiplication and something called "powers" and dodging people at recess to protect my arm (gee, I'd almost forgotten!). I enter the house feeling that I deserve some attention after my bad, but usual day and tell Mama and Nancy how much my arm is killing me. Nancy, a doubting Thomas anyway, says, "Aw, come on." I slink up to my bedroom to pout. My sister always says something to Mama as I pass about how I have a chip on my shoulder. I never know what this means and glance at both shoulders wondering if she sees something that I can't.

The other way home is the shortcut. Generally shortcuts are the way I do everything. Get the job done, even if you have to cut corners. But the shortcut to school isn't easy. There is a barrier of a homemade section of fence between two chain-linked fences. This fence is made of extra thick board about four inches wide. The entire space is about two feet across and four feet high. There is only a small crack between the horizontal boards. That little homemade fence is the only real barrier on the shortcut between my house and school. The way I can get across it, after cursing my eight-year- old curses, is by hobbling over the rough backyard to get there. Then I throw my books over the fence, place my right toe into the tiny space between the boards and throw the left leg over the top.

I hate that fence, and the walk over the grass before and after it, but it gets me to and from school.

When I get home Mama has finished putting the sheets out to dry. I go to my room and daydream about being an important secretary like Ann Southern on the television show. Bored, I go out to play in the yard. Now Mama is burning trash near that big beehive hanging on the back of the deserted school. Both scare me. I don't like the smell of trash burning so I limp across the yard to the clothesline. I love to walk underneath the damp nice smelling sheets that are hanging on the clothesline. I stop to grab a wooden clothespin and put it in my mouth like Mama does when she's hanging the wash. The new plastic ones have little springs and can pinch!

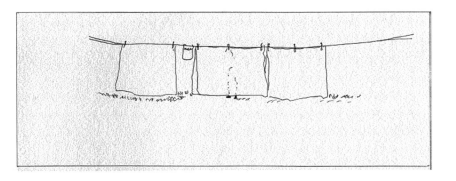

Seven in the Hospital

1958

Last Saturday my Mama told me I have to go to the hospital again. I have to have my tonsils out. I'm very, very scared. We're going to go for the usual prick in my finger at the hospital downtown. They take blood out of my finger two days before I go for surgery. One time they gave me a piece of cotton shaped like my finger with bunny ears on top. I still didn't like the dull, metal thing that they pushed in my finger. I don't know why they don't use something sharper. It looks like a large gray nail that is flat on the part where they push it in me. It hurts!

The weekend before I go, my Mama says we can buy a new nightie for my stay in the hospital. We go to Jelleff's to look for one. They are all really pretty. Some are silky pink or blue. Some are soft cotton in different colors. I pick out a light blue one but I still don't like the idea of having to buy it so I can go to the hospital! I want it all to be over! I can't stop thinking about what it will be like. I always remember the sickening sweet smell of the ether coming through the rubber mask over my face. I know that's when I will feel like I'm dying…like they are killing me against my will. When I watch movies or shows on TV about the killing of the Jewish people in the war, I think this is what it is like. I really hope I don't scream like last time when I go into the waiting room before they put me to sleep. I want Mama to be proud of me this time, so I will really, really try not to cry or tell her how I feel no matter how scared I am.

I behaved a little better this time but Mama says I squeezed her hand too tight. Just before they took me down for surgery they gave me something to calm me down so I "wouldn't care" they said. When I woke up Mama was there on the left side of my bed and brought over the cutest thing she bought at the gift shop. It was nighttime. I was very sleepy and my throat was sore and I threw up a lot. The gift Mama brought was a little doll house chest of drawers with an oval mirror in it and a little red ribbon to pull open a little drawer. It was the best gift I ever got! I also had a big patch over my right eye when I woke up. I couldn't remember right away that just before they put me to sleep I noticed my eye doctor standing at the end of the stretcher in the surgery room. My regular doctor, Dr. Weber, was on the right side of the stretcher. I looked at Dr. Costenbader and said, "What are you doing here?"

And he said," We thought we'd kill 2 birds with one stone." They both had their white masks over their mouth.

I don't think I was mad but I sure was surprised. I knew they were talking about giving me eye surgery but I didn't know it was now! I didn't have time to think about how cousin Stuart says they take your eye out and put it on your cheek while they cut the muscle so your eye doesn't cross anymore. I found out later that this is exactly what they did!

I felt horrible but they brought me ice cream. So that part is true. They really *do* bring you ice cream when they take out your tonsils. I got lonely in the dark cold room when I slept each night. It felt like being in jail. I *hate* when they take my temperature or give me more shots.

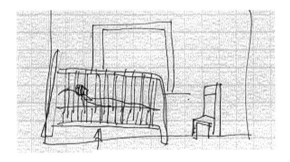

Two days after my operations, as usual, they push me in a wheelchair out front where Daddy brings the car right in front of the hospital to pick me up. It was sunny. I'm so glad it's over. I don't want to do this anymore!

Summer

1958

Finishing the second grade seems like no accomplishment at all since Laurel has just finished the third but summer is almost here.

The last day of school is *so* exciting! I finally get to take home my papers and art work. All year the teacher was hoarding these for display on the bulletin board and in the hall next to the principal's office. I never saw any of my stuff on either though I thought myself the best of artists. The classroom is a mess. Papers and trash cover the floor. Old broken chewed-on pencils, an old construction paper valentine heart, Christmas candy, and broken rulers. The teacher is calling out our names to pick up old book reports, drawings and arithmetic homework. I toss out the C's and C-'s and keep the C+'s and B-'s. She also hands out the last of the rubberbands so that we can roll up our artwork to take home. When the bell rings to end school we all try to run out of the school but we creep since our arms are laden down with macaroni shell-studded shoe box jewelry boxes for Mom and crayon and tempera paint pictures for Dad's office. By the time I get home, most everything is destroyed, wrinkled and dirty from being dropped so many times on the way. The rolled-up papers have somehow become bent in half. Little do I know that these treasures will all be lost forever in a few days.

Summer is the same as weekends only more boring. The highlight, or exception, is Daddy's two weeks vacation because that means it's our vacation. Most years we go to Georgia to see my grandparents and other relatives on my mother's side. The trip is a six hundred mile, two-day fight with my sister and strained tensions between all of us. The trip and the visit are very, very hot as neither air conditioned cars nor homes were invented. Despite the heat, the visit at Mama Sara's and Daddy Faye's is always quite enjoyable. I love the wonderful rhythmic sound of tree frogs every night while lying in the little guest bed. I feel self-conscious kneeling by the bed for prayers with my cousins. We never do it at home.

That is how we spend one of the weeks of Dad's vacation. The other is at Colonial Beach, Virginia, at my aunt and uncle's beach cottages. The "front" cottage faces the river. The "back" cottage is directly behind the front cottage with a little yard and hammock in between. Both cottages are very old, with cracked vinyl floors and a musty smell.

We arrive late at night, as my uncle has to work late at his dentistry. We drag our gear to the front cottage and the folks set up our cots on the front screened-in porch. My cousin and I happily pick from the pile of old army cot blankets and cut-to-size sheets. We each have our favorite set. I always bring my own pillow as my piece of security from home.

Front porch/cots, Front Cottage
Colonial Beach, Va.

    The first night there, Laurel and I play cards or read the tired old comic books from the huge box of them located in the antique bureau in the living room. The men are sitting slouched, a relaxed slouch, in the living room talking about how "glorious" it is here, on the polluted, jelly fish-ridden Potomac River near the Chesapeake Bay. To them the food always tastes better, they sleep and feel better when the only difference between here and home is that this is here and home is there. This place even smells worse and looks worse than home and there isn't even any television. But we love it, too. Everyone gets along with each other much better here.

Looking Out of Front Cottage
toward Potomac
Colonial Beach, Va.

Front Cottage/Back bedroom-Looking
thru back porch to back Cottage
Colonial Beach, Va.

  During the day the men are off in the boat (we get to go later), mowing
the grass, playing croquet or cooking hickory-smoked barbecue chicken on the
grill for dinner.

  Laurel and I are up at 9 or 10 o'clock the next morning. There is still
enough batter, and an adult still sitting at the table, to make our pancakes. The
griddle is a fantastic antique griddle that plugs into the light on the tiny back
porch where we eat. Sometimes when the table is crowded the only way to get
into the porch is to climb through the back bedroom window where my cousin
Stuart and Jay usually sleep. They are teenagers and sleep really late. They
mutter obscenities as we tromp through the room and climb through the
window, giggling, and onto the bench to eat our perfectly-made pancakes.
Even when the porch is empty this is a fun way to enter the porch!

  Next we walk to the boardwalk for more comic books, some candy, and
another sand pail, (the ones from last year are rusty) and a delicious snow cone.
On the way back we stop to play on an old cannon.

  We take turns in the front cottage bathroom getting into our bathing
suits. The bathroom is odd but pleasant with its clawfoot tub and cracked vinyl
flooring. The odd part is you literally have to walk up to the john because the
floor is slanted. The tub drains rapidly. The drain is at the low end of the room.

This is the only bathroom I have ever been in that has a rubber hose thingie to use as a "shower". There is always sand on the vinyl and wood floors in both cottages as well as in the tub, which is scratchy to sit on while bathing!

Bathroom, Front Cottage
Colonial Beach, Va.

When in our suits, we walk over the gum burrs (ouch!), across the street and down the steep path to the beach, the murky water and the jellyfish. Laurel catches a few of the latter and drags them on to the beach to show me how you can't get stung if you walk on them in your bare feet! What a mystery. She is either brave or crazy, I think. She then covers them with sand but I make wide circles all around them to get back to my beach towel, not trusting her demonstration.

Later, it begins to drizzle. Dinnertime is approaching so the parents decide we should all go to Wilkerson's, one of two seafood restaurants in the area. The barbecue chicken cookout is postponed. After a dinner of mallet pounding crabs on brown paper and key lime pie we return to the cottage miserably stuffed but happy. Laurel and I again open the living room bureau and dig out old cardboard puzzle boxes. We select the puzzle with the German castle in the fall. All will participate in this activity for the rest of the week, passing by the card table and exclaiming aloud when they match two pieces. Some will be found silently bent over the table for long periods. Initially the outer edges are found and then each person will somehow work on their "own" area. One or two will work only on the sky, another on the trees, another on the clouds and another on the castle. I think these choices say a lot about the intellect of the person, but I'm not sure what. Uncle Jimmy would pick the most miserable part of the puzzle such as the sky and use his special dental glasses with those extenders to do it.

Bedtime is usually welcome except this is when I realize I'm horribly sunburned. Mama tries to put Noxzema on my shoulders as I whine with each touch. I actually glow with heat. Now the army blankets don't sound too good, as they are wool and scratchy. I also am beginning to itch from some mosquito bites or "skeeters" as my Georgian mother calls them.

Some people actually see the mosquito as it lights on their body. Not me. It's like I generate the welts myself. I *never* see them but sometimes I hear them. I wonder why I don't see them because when I look at the bare yellow light bulb in the porch ceiling they are as big as hummingbirds! During their dance, once they slip indoors, they cast really long shadows. I receive the bites, I guess, while I am in motion, oblivious to them until I begin to see the low white mesas form on my arms and legs. They are not small reactions but truly mesa-like structures that shock those that see them. The scratching from the ones I receive today will last for days. I will then look like I have leprosy but it will get much better.

Sometimes it is hard to sleep on the porch because I'm always so excited to be here! When I can't sleep I listen to the green thatch blinds just over my cot creaking in the strong breeze. If I can't sleep, I sit up on my cot and quietly roll up the blinds enough to peek out at the water. I can feel a cool breeze on my face and hear the waves rolling on to the shore that get louder as the tide comes in. I can see the lights on the other shore or a single light going up and down the river. You can't see the boat, just the light. When it rains and blows real hard, parents come out and pick up the cots and put them in the living room. When it is only a light rain, I like how it gets cooler and the screens smell metally. (Mama will say that you can smell the rain comin'. I think she smells the screens as it starts to rain.)

Last time, the boys slept under the front side of the porch, under the blinds. My cot was on the side without any blinds, which is okay because I can look at the stars while I am lying down. I think about how good life is and wonder what life will be like when I grow up. This is when I "night dream" but am not asleep. When I daydream it's different.

Last year we went in the backyard between the two cottages and watched for Sputnik. We saw the little light float by in the sky and everyone was surprised but not happy. Sputnik was made by the Russians.

Gratitude

1997

The black stuff of depression has a large sucking sound you know. It pulls and yanks and mostly succeeds at frightening you with its overwhelming power. Until you step away physically from where it got you for a little or a long while. It helps. Try it. But go see some other human if you can. Plan your time with others ahead and then add your life to theirs for awhile. You shall be healed for a while. Hug and pet your pets with gusto, to melt the pain. Get perspective, distance, out of the death grip of the awful thing. It lurks in the corners and walls of where you last felt it. But you can exorcise it with good thoughts. Like the time that the grocery store cashier came around the counter to give me a hug when I mentioned that my husband died. And the time the cab driver smiled cheerfully when confronted with two people, a wheelchair, two suitcases, three smaller cases, and a huge canvas bag to fit in his vehicle. And he did it with great finesse and a posture of joy, of all things!

And the work friends from across the country that call just to say hello when they know I am having a rough time. The warm hug of my son as he is leaving to go back to school saying how much he'll miss me. The car that lets you into a heavy line of traffic. The stranger that very quietly tells you that your skirt isn't zipped. The feelings of joy when you see someone you love after some time has gone by. Sunset in Monument Valley, Arizona. Early, misty mornings on any ocean, river or bay on a sunny day. A handwritten letter in the mailbox. The ironic sense of unity and freedom that comes from nowhere on an insanely crowded freeway while the music blares on the radio.

The joy of helping a mentally ill person successfully find their gate at an airport. The soothed feeling that can come from being with quiet children when you just feel like crap. Fleeting feelings of being somehow still loved by my dead husband. The sound of my children giggling half the night while I lay in the dark. Watching my cat lick my dog on the nose, or the head or the ear or the toes. Listening to my cat purr while lying heavily on my chest.

Having clean clothes. Lying in a warm, comfortable bed. Having a garage. Water running from the faucet on command. Starry cold nights.

Thanks God.

Nana, My Next Door Neighbor

1959

When we get back from Colonial Beach it is only Saturday. While everyone is putting things away I go to my Nana's house next door. I climb the little wooden gray steps at the back of her house. I can feel the gray, chipped paint as I hold the rail. I never need to knock on the door. Sometimes I sit in the little bright red vinyl chair in the kitchen and my Nana and I talk for a long time. I watch her back while she makes bread out of that big blue metal can with pure white stuff inside. I think she puts it in a bowl but I can't see what she's doing while we talk. When she's finished, she sits down awhile and says, "The dough needs to rise," and points to a kitchen towel over top of the bowl. I love the smell of the towel after the dough rises. I just put my face in that warm towel. Nana says I smell the yeast.

I feel real hot with the oven on in here and my legs stick to the vinyl chair. Nana says I should stop talking and take my two thumbs and push my front teeth together while I sit here. I have a big gap between my front teeth. I try so hard that I make dents in my thumbs!

Later on, my sister and I will sleep upstairs in Nana's house while Mama and Daddy go dancin'. They take dance lessons at Art Murry's house I think. Just before we go to bed, Nana asks us if we want a nice slice of her warm baked bread. We get a choice of butter all over the bread and sugar on top or lots of butter and peanut butter. I switch each time. Both kinds make me get real sick at my stomach after I go to bed. I really miss my Mama and Daddy when I stay here, too. But Nana tells us stories. I sleep in the little bed under the slanted ceiling and Nancy sleeps in the other bed across the room. Nana sits on the end of my bed and tells us both stories and how she doesn't want to be sick and lose her mind when she gets really old. *(This really happened later, when she had a bad stroke. She lived for lots of years in a nursing home, almost like a "vegetable" my Dad says).*

Between saying our bedtime prayers and Nana's stories I usually get real nauseated. I get so scared that something might happen to my mama and daddy. Nana puts a little trashcan by the bed "just in case" I have to be sick. I don't like it when she leaves because when she is talking it doesn't make me feel as sick. She puts the hall light on and leaves the door open when I feel like this. She says goodnight and tells me to use the trashcan if I feel like upchucking. That's a funny word. My friends say "throw-up". Upchuck sounds like a little furry animal.

I never have gotten sick here because after Nana leaves, I count the green ivy leaves in the wallpaper to get my mind off how I feel. I pretend Mama and Daddy are already home and don't want to bring us home so we can have our fun time with Nana. Nana is my daddy's mother. He never calls her Mama or Mom, just Mother. He only calls my grandfather "Father". These grandparents are different than my grandparents in Georgia. I think my grandparents next door are smart and ritch!

    When I get up the next day Nana makes me take a bath. I like to take a bath here because it is different than our bathroom and sunny, too. It smells real clean. I don't like the way my grandparent's bathroom smells downstairs. It smells like the stuff my grandfather, Papa Paul, puts his teeth in. One time Nana made me wash my mouth out with soap in there when I said something bad!

    Nana and Papa Paul's bedroom has two single beds and green ivy wallpaper, too. The boards at the head of the bed are made of gray, plushy smooth leathery stuff with brass tacks on the front all around the curvy edges. There is a big oval framed thing on the wall by Nana's bed. It scares me. It looks like a dead brown upside down wreath under glass. Nana says it is a very expensive wreath of brown human hair! I don't like it.

NANA's & PAPA PAUL's BEDROOM
119 N. Fairfax St. Falls Church, V

Airport Story

1997

With much anticipation I was heading to Atlanta to see my daughter, Sarah, for the weekend. She had started her first job after graduation and moved into her first apartment. I wanted to spend time with her at her new abode. She had made nice plans for us and I had purchased a reasonably-priced ticket.

My plane was due to depart Dulles at 4:30 p.m., and I arrived there sometime after 3 o'clock. The sign indicated the plane was on time, no delays. I had been reading for awhile when they announced the plane was delayed leaving Rochester, New York, due to storms. Perhaps a twenty-minute delay. I have been here before. Just hang out, it will double.

After about an hour, I tried to reach Sarah but, unfortunately, the voicemail at her work was out so I couldn't leave a message. I knew she would check the plane's status before leaving for the long ride to the airport. After walking around a while feeling low and lonely, for some reason I said a little prayer request to lift the yuck feeling. Since the delay was now estimated at two hours, I decided I would make an effort, though painful, to say something nice to someone.

I sat down next to a woman in a very bright green walking outfit. I commented on the pretty color of her suit. In a foreign accent, she said she thought it was turquoise. I asked her where she is from, and she said Ethiopia. She had been trying to get to Atlanta from LA for several days to spend time with her brother. But flying stand-by was making it difficult, spending the previous night in Chicago when she could not get a flight here. She wondered if she would get on the flight to Atlanta. She seemed resigned to her situation and, obviously, weary.

I listened while she spoke of a trip to Washington two years ago to be with her mother, who while visiting the area, had become ill and died at a local hospital. She began to cry a little. I told her about my mother's passing twenty-two years ago and my husband just three years ago. We talked about how irreplaceable they are, how short life is, etc. This was all we spoke.

I tried to call Sarah again, hopeful that she had not decided to go to the airport as the incoming plane was now not due at Dulles until 8:50 p.m. (a four-hour delay). No answer. The time to visit Sarah was shortening. My return flight was early Sunday.

I tried to call Sarah at her home, but she wasn't there. I turned on my cell phone and she called me just then from her home. We discussed the pros and cons of my coming or waiting until a later date. We decided to give up this visit. I really didn't want her coming to the airport alone so late (~11p.m.), and she stubbornly wouldn't let me take a cab. So sadly, but wisely, I said I would reschedule. When I turned in my boarding pass at the desk, the agent asked if I knew any Spanish. "Un poco," I said. They handed me an elderly couple and their tickets.

The wife was in a wheelchair and there was an airport assistant, a man, pushing the wheelchair. The husband was looking frustrated and confused. The name on the tickets was Miramelli. I assumed it was their name, or so it would seem, and their next stop would be Milan, Italy. I asked if they were the Miramelli's and they said "No, no." Their names, they said, were Sancha, Alfredo and Maria. I said to the person at the desk, "This isn't their ticket!" He said he knew that and, without looking up, he brushed me off. I suggested we all go to the customer service desk. As we headed in that direction, the wife, Maria, said a woman had taken them to the gate for Atlanta, taken their ticket and *boarding passes* and left. The elderly couple said they thought the woman's name was Doris. They did not know they were given back someone else's tickets.

They had been scheduled to leave for Miami two hours earlier to meet their daughter who had flown from Santiago, Chile, their home and final destination. The Sancha's had flown to Dulles that morning from Paris via New York and had been trying to make their connection. They spoke some English but it took about thirty minutes to discern all of the above. The man behind the wheelchair said to me, "God will bless you for this, nice lady."

The three of us (four, including the man pushing the wheelchair) arrived at the customer service desk, which was very busy due to delays and cancellations throughout the northeast. I asked the man at the desk (another foreign nationality, perhaps from India...still no one to speak Spanish?!) to page the *real* Miramelli's for their lost ticket and *please* help these people. He spoke through me to the husband, Alfredo, for the most part and vice versa but it was a mighty struggle. Maria was very concerned about her daughter waiting and so we arranged to have her paged in Miami. As we told the story, the customer service agent remembered seeing the couple earlier at the desk and that Annette (not Doris) had been helping them. He paged Annette but she didn't respond, so he agreed to walk with us to try and find her at the gate. He found her, but she had no recollection of bringing them there or how they had gotten someone else's ticket. Neither I, nor the fellow pushing the wheelchair, believed her. We all headed back to the customer service desk. Again, the man behind the wheelchair said in his broken English, "God will bless you for this".

When we got back to the desk I asked Alfredo if I could go through his briefcase just to be sure the tickets weren't there. We found the tickets from Miami to Santiago. That was good news. Their daughter called back, so more good news. The man at the desk now found the Sancha's itinerary in the computer but he needed a receipt to reissue tickets. I figured if the tickets to Santiago were in the briefcase, there should also be a receipt. So again I asked Alfredo if I could look in his briefcase. He was trying valiantly to be the good man and husband taking care of matters, but he was frustrated probably due to fatigue and the language barrier. He nodded to indicate it was okay for me to recheck his case. Bingo, receipts…more good news! The customer service man began to issue new tickets for 5:40 p.m. the next day non-stop to Miami. He also issued vouchers for a hotel, taxi, phone and food.

During much of this translating, talking, and sometimes shouting - as you do when you can't get the language - I sensed us being watched by the group in line for a long time next to us. Maria, relieved, asked for my name and address, so we exchanged cards. The man driving the wheelchair opened his wallet and staring at it said, "I have no card to exchange." Then he paused, looked down and said, "I only have pictures of my wife, two daughters and three sons…. all killed by Saddam, two years and five months ago". He began to cry so hard that he went to his knees. When he stood up, wiping his tears, he pulled gently at his airport uniform vest and said to me, "This is not my job. This is not who I am. I was a poet who wrote in four languages in Iraq. I do not know why I am still here."

Just then I knew exactly what he meant. He couldn't understand why he was still alive. I couldn't relate to his horrible tragedy, but I could relate to his last words. I had thought and said those same words to myself many times after my husband Jim died, and my children had gone off to college, all at the same time. Why *was* I still here? For what purpose? Now I knew what I could say to him. "This is why you are still here. For moments just like this. Your job helps people all day long."

Meanwhile, Maria was poking at me: "What is wrong, what is wrong?"

I told her, "His familia es muerte. Iraqi. Saddam's hombres." She shook her head, "Oh, no. Oh, no." This man had been with them for six hours so far.

While we were waiting for the vouchers, the couple repeated several times that all ten of their children are professionals in business, including one son who is president of a bank in Miami. I think they wanted me to know they weren't just stupid or lost and saying this would convince me. They were going to see this son and a daughter in Miami before returning to Santiago. The couple went on to share that earlier this same day they had been in a cab accident on their way to DeGaulle airport.

For some reason I felt the need to go back one last time to my gate to see if their tickets had been found or returned at the desk. The plane I was supposed to be taking to Atlanta had arrived and was boarding. Two women in line spoke to me. One said, "Aren't you coming? Where have you been?" I told her I wasn't going to Atlanta. It was too late for my daughter and a waste. The other came over to tell me she was glad I was helping the older couple because no one helped them at the desk.

While checking for the Sancha's tickets at the desk, the woman in green from Ethiopia was finally getting her boarding ticket for Atlanta. The woman behind the desk was telling her that earlier a woman turned in her boarding pass (that was me!) and she could now board the plane. I said to the woman in green, "That's terrific, I really *wasn't* meant to go to Atlanta."

After Alfredo had all the vouchers and ticket in his briefcase, I suggested we go to the taxi stand. I needed to go there to get home anyway. Just before exiting the building, I asked Alfredo to get out the taxi voucher. He'd already forgotten where he'd put things. So again he let me go search in his briefcase. I then put the hotel, food and phone vouchers in his jacket pocket and the ticket back in the briefcase. Holding the taxi voucher high, I said, "*Now* we can go!"

The wheelchair man pushed forward to the front of the long taxi line. After the last episode I thought, "What the heck, I'll make sure that they get to the hotel and checked in and take another taxi home from there." Alfredo and Maria gratefully hugged the "useless" wheelchair man and we got into the taxi.

We arrived at the Hyatt in Reston and the smiling Alfredo let me get the hotel voucher from his jacket (we laughed about that…totally punchy at this point) and they were checked in. They asked me to stay for dinner, but it was 11 o'clock. They were probably exhausted and I wanted to get home, so I declined. As I was about to leave I thought, "Wouldn't it be horrible if they had more problems tomorrow?" I told them I would come back at 3 o'clock the next day to accompany them to the airport and the right gate. They seemed to like the idea. I had nothing better to do.

Saturday, I met them in the lobby, got the other taxi voucher (Alfredo handed it to me this time) and asked the concierge to hail a cab. I still had a disposable camera in my purse for the Atlanta trip and asked them if I could take their picture. They were a very, very handsome couple.

I learned more about them as we traveled to the airport. Alfredo is age seventy-eight and still works ten hours a day. They had just come from Paris after a two-week seminar on wine. He said they were the third generation owners of vineyards and a fruit export company. When I got home that evening, I discovered on the Internet that the wine is a world-famous Chilean wine.

After checking their bags at the airport counter, Maria had to go through security in the wheelchair through a separate door, while Alfredo and I went through the standard screen. As Alfredo and I exited, he began to move quickly away toward the busses thinking that Maria had already passed through. I moved rapidly to catch up to him, then told him to wait as she had not come through. I was feeling glad that I came.

We got to the gate and I said to them, "We shall not move!" They were ecstatic when they saw the matching flight number and the word "Miami" appear on the board at the gate. Only one more incident: when we heard shouting across the way at the bar, Alfredo couldn't resist investigating. The World Cup soccer games were being televised, and Brazil was playing Chile. Though he was oblivious to us, I promised Maria I would keep an eye on him. Just before boarding he wandered back. I felt a great sense of relief watching them board. I had made wonderful, though temporary friends. They should not have been traveling alone and I was glad that their daughter would be meeting them in Miami.

When I called Sarah to tell her what had happened, she told me about her own unplanned adventure in Atlanta. She and a friend had searched restaurants until 1 o'clock in the morning for ten-pound empty cans. The next day she would help her friend teach a music and art class for inner city kids at the High Gallery. They needed twenty-five large cans to make musical instruments with the children.

The moral of the story is just too obvious. It was an amazing experience.

Postscript: About ten days after the airport encounter, I received a package at my office. It was a beautiful porcelain angel that plays the song "My Hero" and a lovely note from Maria, written in broken English.

Winter Play

1958

I love the big snowstorms in my town, especially when school closes. This winter we had a *really, really* big snowstorm and my Daddy shoveled so much snow that he hurt his shoulder and had to go to bed for days. That's also when the power went out. He was upstairs and when the wind came and blew the snow all over, we had no lights or TV! So my mama, sister and me put blankets, sheets and our pillows down in front of the fireplace and had a fire. It was fun except that Daddy was upstairs with lots and lots of blankets on him while his shoulder hurt. We can't even get him to the doctor because the snow is two feet deep and our car is just a big white lump in the driveway!

I'm not complaining too much, but when the snow melted some, I wanted to go out and play. But it's hard for me to get around out there. My mama and me get real irritated at each other. Yesterday she was trying to help me but things didn't work out too good. First she put my snowsuit on and told me to lay down while she put a plastic dry cleaning bag over my brace and brace shoe with a rubber band. The shoe costs a lot of money and she didn't want it to get wet. The rubber band is a little too tight against my ankle but I wanna go play in a hurry so I don't say anything to Mama. Mama helps me stand up cuz the snowsuit doesn't let me bend too well! Then she hands me my pointy wool hat and my mittens. I put them on and start to walk to the side door near the kitchen: crinkle, crinkle, crinkle. I feel pretty hot in all of this stuff and can't wait to go out where it's *cold*!

When I get outside it is so, so bright that I can barely see for a minute or so. I walk a few steps and rrripppp, the plastic breaks over the brace and a WHOLE bunch of snow gets in it. As I walk back to the door calling for Mama more snow gets inside the plastic and it is real heavy to drag it back. Mama looks kinda frowny behind the storm door. I step just inside the door and she takes it off. The snow makes a big mess on the floor. Mama tells me I can try to play for a while without the shoe being covered. So I go back out feeling happy about this! There is one problem with not having a boot on the left foot. As I walk I collect about an inch on the bottom of the warm sole of the brace so I have to stop every few feet and push it off so I can keep going! I wish I could have two red rubber boots even though you still get snow down in the regular boot and it is *cold*! My left foot is real high off the ground so this doesn't happen.

I like to be pulled on our wooden sled but I am a little scared because the front part pinches sometimes. Nancy and her friend Nancy (they have the same name) pull me. I like it best when it is dark and Daddy takes us sledding right on our street. The snow looks really pretty when the streetlights are on. It feels cozy instead of cold. It's real, real quiet except for the sound of the sled on the snow and our giggling. Daddy looks funny when he gets on the sled because he is so big. He seems to have a lot of fun sledding with us.

I hope I get new winter clothes for Christmas. The scarf I wear goes over my head and ties in a little knot under my chin. It is wool and so, so scratchy! Some kids have a hood on their coats. I have a car coat and a snowsuit. I like the brown, wooden buttons on my car coat because they look like little barrels. My sister got a new camel hair coat but Mama says it isn't made out of real camel hair.

Christmas was happy this year. I got a one-year diary.

January 4th
I'm getting 1-tooth pulled this morning by Dr. Mead. Only a whiff of gas. Mama says not to be scared. I can't go to school again! Tomorrow I'm going to use part of my allowance to get an everyday purse. I didn't like having my tooth pulled. It's big. The car broke down today and Mama had to take a taxi home from the Safeway.

January 7th
I am at school. I had lots of homework. Nancy has two more warts. Next Tuesday I am going to Dr. Curtis to check my teeth. I got my new purse today. It's exactly like Laurel's. I love it. Mama has bridge tomorrow night. Mama drove me home today. Daddy has been real sweet tonight. Mama is normal (that's sweet). Heat is off.

February 2nd
I've got a cavity on 1 of the teeth that show when I smile! It kind of hurts. I wish I wasn't such a worrywart. It's ridiculous. The Lord will take care of any problem I have but we solve it ourselves in such a way I can't explain. History test was kind of hard. I'm getting a "C" in Science! "B's" in ESG. Some grades went up, some down. Some stayed. Mike Sullivan has been talking to Carol P. She tells me he says I liked him. I wonder if we'll ever talk again. A lot of homework tonight. Dear Lord forgive my sins.

Meeting Ice in Rosslyn

1996

Work at a Fortune 500 company is pretty much like any other large company. There are lots of meetings. They take on a life of their own. Many meetings have little substance and no outcome. Mostly, they provide a way of communicating. Whoever is leading it has the power. But, ah, the project reviews. They take a lot of preparation by the projects and are awful to watch if the reviewer is an SOB. But this story isn't about that kind of review.

Some time just before or after Jim died, I was asked to evaluate an aerospace project that was in trouble. For the first seventeen years or so, I was a worker, then manager, and then a briefer to the erstwhile management du jour. When I received that first phone call from the retiring vice president of finance to investigate a problem, it didn't strike me as something I'd waited for my whole career. It didn't feel like a sign that I'd *arrived*. I just answered the phone and said I would be glad to go check it out.

While I didn't recognize this as the first step of a six-year mile, I decided as I drove north around the beltway, it was kind of neat to be asked. Maybe I had some value after all. After I completed my written evaluation with recommendations, of course, I went back to my current assignment. At that time I was helping to define the requirements for a database information system our organization would use on projects. (The organization is about 15,000 employees, post a couple of Pac-man-like acquisitions, and part of a $17 billion company.)

A year or so later, I was asked by the vice president of programs to accompany him on a project review in Rosslyn, Virginia, just across the Potomac from Georgetown and Washington, D.C. Hereinafter he will be referred to as "Dr. Bob" (just a PhD).

This fellow's homeroom was Los Angeles, California. The first thing he wanted to know was if I knew where a special pen place was located in Georgetown so we could stop there on the way to or from the review. "A pin place?" I asked. I knew I hadn't heard him right but thought he might be looking to buy a gift, like a broch, or a place to repair one.

"No," he said. "A place where you buy really, really good pens, the ones with ink!" Odd, I thought, and told him I had never heard of the place and wasn't familiar with its location. I lived close to the beltway back then, and he was lodged in a nearby hotel. He proposed that I meet him in his hotel's lobby, he would drive us to the meeting in Rosslyn.

I woke up that morning to a lot of "ticking" on the window…like sleet, like *ice*. I am not usually daunted or fearful of driving in bad weather having lived in the Washington area most of my life. Knowing the weather wouldn't make the drive quick or easy, I left a little early for the hotel. I carried my umbrella with me.

When I arrived, Dr. Bob was jaunting through the lobby. Dr. Bob was in his mid-fifties, obviously bright, *very* direct in his communication and seemingly a pretty happy fellow. Once we got to his rental car in the garage, he said he liked staying at this hotel, although far from the office, since it had a good gym. He also said, "You have really shitty weather in Washington." Opinionated, I thought to myself.

Neither of us had been to this particular facility, so we wandered off track a bit as we entered Rosslyn. Rosslyn is built on a river bluff (the dear Potomac's). It is a compact mini-city with lots of high rises built close together on little hills. The streets intersect at odd angles, curve and some dead-end. Dr. Bob had some general directions to a parking garage. We located the building where the meeting would be held on a dead end street and proceeded to find the garage. Well, it actually wasn't close at all to where our meeting would be held, and it was still sleeting. We were pushing the start time, but I didn't say anything about dropping me off at the building because I was sure the garage wouldn't be too far. Well, in Rosslyn for a crip like me in the ice, it was *faaarr*! Dr. Bob obviously was oblivious. Most people are after they meet me. They soon forget about my appearance, which is fine except for instances like this one. I've sucked it up before, so I said nothing. We began the trek in the ice. Not only was it falling from the sky, but ice had formed where the tires had previously slogged through slush. So crossing streets was tricky. Dr. Bob was about twenty feet ahead of me and probably talking to me. I think he finally looked back and said, "Hurry up!"

I said something like, "Darnit, slow down!" But I probably really said, 'I'm comin', I'm comin'!" I could have used an arm in a couple places, but like I said I've done this before.

When we finally arrived we were about ten minutes late. The waiting receptionist quickly checked our badges and ushered us into the large conference room. We both knew the project manager who called out to Dr. Bob, "Bob, where have you been?" He was walking down the left aisle in the room of about fifty people, while I walked down the right.

As he walked he answered, "You didn't tell me the parking garage was blocks away!" Well, I thought. At least after this scene he'll pick me up at the door when we leave! We landed at the front table where a couple other "reviewers" were seated and I relaxed. Things were fine until during one of the presentations, Dr. Bob started talking to another reviewer (another VP). How rude! I thought. Is this a ploy because he doesn't like the presentation? I've seen odd tactics like this when I was part of a team of briefers myself. But he and the other fellow kept talking, kind of huddled together. I leaned over to see what they were doing. They were talking in normal voices (not whispering) while comparing their beloved fountain pens! Dr. Bob appeared indifferent to the presenter. I later found out that he was an only child. Ah, only child syndrome! I thought to myself. Only-children often aren't tuned-in to others' feelings. It helped to know this, though the revelation was a little late.

But something about Dr. Bob was just too funny and hard to describe. I expressed my irritation, but oddly, I wasn't mad at him. Of course, the review was supposed to be really important. As you can tell, I only remembered these parts. That's the way most of these meetings would be…lots of talk, little substance. While the meetings helped communicate status and issues, I think they really were another way to justify their and our existence!

Years later I heard that Dr. Bob was sharing the ice story with his friends and co-workers. No, he didn't pick me up at the door when the meeting was over. We slopped and slogged back to the car, him telling me to hurry up. But we didn't go to the pen place.

"Hollywood"

Naval Inspection (1960) - About once a year we all go to the airbase when Daddy is doing the naval inspection. What happens is we get all dressed up. Mama wears her pretty brown hat with matching brown dress, matching round brown purse and matching brown shoes. This is odd for Mama. Normally she wears her shorts and golf socks and tennis shoes. Even in winter she wears wool shorts and a sweatshirt. Mama is an athlete. She taught tennis, fencing and archery in college and at girl's camps when she was a camp counselor. Mama plays golf at least three or four times a week at the country club. Sometimes she can't play golf because she gets a call to be a substitute teacher for phys-ed or French. She sounds funny when she speaks French with a Georgia accent. Her Daddy's name is Lafayette. We call him Daddy Faye. He is deaf and I have to write him notes when we "talk".

I get to wear my new white gloves to navy inspection. This is the third time I can remember going to this. I find it boring because it is long. But it's exciting, too, because my daddy is in charge. He wears his "dress blue" uniform with a white hat with "scrambled eggs" on the front (that's what he calls them). He wears his sword, too. When he is inspecting the "troops" he walks up and down in front of many types of navy men with his head straight ahead: up and down, up and down the lines in the really large hangar at the air base. We sit on the bleachers. I think it is really sad that the sailors sometimes faint right in line because they have to stand at attention for so long. It is very, very hot in there, too. My daddy doesn't seem like a mean person. But I think it's mean to make those men stand for so long in the huge hot hangar while we watch. I don't know why they do this. But Mama says it is very important. Afterward, Daddy introduces my mama, my sister and me to the admirals. My daddy is a captain. He is also a pilot and flies on weekends. I think he is embarrassed to have them meet me. I'm not perfect, just like those sailors. I don't understand why my dad also inspects the lines of sailors. My daddy always makes sure everyone knows he is a navy airman.

Mr. Nixon at the Station (1958) - I feel very proud that my daddy is real important. Just like at the TV station where he works. One time Nana and I watched daddy on TV at her house when he was showing what a navy survival suit looks like by wearing it and describing all the pockets. Daddy has worked for radio and TV for a real long time. I think my daddy is famous. He knows a lot of famous people like Willard Scott, Carol Channing, Nanette Fabaret and Bob Hope. My mama told me she liked Charles Laughton at a party because he seemed like a normal person. I have an autograph from Rod Serling my dad got once when he had lunch with him. He is the guy on the Twilight Zone TV show. I'm real lucky. This stuff is important and I like the way my friends are interested in me talking about it.

One Sunday, Daddy needed to pick up something at the TV station after church and we went into the lobby to wait for him. I had on my gloves then, too. On the right side of the lobby next to the case with all the awards, a man came over to shake my hand. My mama says it was Mr. Nixon. When mama told me he was running for president I said I wouldn't wash that glove ever again! She said he had just finished something called a debate in one of the studios. He has a dog named Checkers that looks just like my dog, Penny! My favorite part of visiting my dad's work is Christmas when all of us kids get a present in one of the studios. Santa is there. Daddy knows I don't believe in Santa anymore so he told me the Santa was really Willard Scott.

One of my daddy's other friends, Jim Henson, at the station does coffee commercials with his puppets. Daddy says he'll never make much money. The puppet in the commercial looks like a green cloth frog with wires you can see moving his arms.

We are the first people in our neighborhood to get a color TV. It is real big with doors that close over the TV. My dad says it is a beautiful piece of furniture. But we got that at the old house on Fairfax Street. We just moved to a real big house on a cul de sac. Daddy now works for the government but does TV stuff. He got a whole lot of money when he left the TV station.

Mama and I laughed when the interior decorator came to make our new living room "ready for entertaining". The nice man kept throwing different colored pillows on to our new couch. We picked the pink ones. He also picked out a real, real, real fancy thing for over the couch. It has a dimmer switch with six lights that look like candles coming out of six large gold stems with gold leaves. It is called a sconce. Daddy says people will be very impressed with how perfect the house looks. They even bought a real pink marble table and crystal lamps with gold cupids holding up the lamp and long icicle like glass things that hang all around the top. It all is very expensive and will mean a lot to our friends. I told my sister about the new stuff but that I really wish I got to see Mama and Daddy more.

Death at the Door (literally) or Beware of Sharper Knives!

1999

My sister and I had just returned from North Carolina where we had spent four days sorting and packing my departed stepmother, Marian's, belongings. My Dad said he couldn't handle the chore by himself.

When we arrived, however, we saw that he had catalogued all of her belongings into neat piles: sweaters, socks, coats, suits, slacks, shorts, expensive blouses, expensive dresses, inexpensive blouses and dresses, etc. We were overwhelmed with what he had done and what we still had left to do. A tough moment was finding one of those mink thingies with five critters' (mink animals) heads biting each other to create a neck wrap. Must have been her mother's. I told Dad to keep this for later. Nightmares.

My sister, being a careful, thorough gal started off the next day by holding up each and every piece of clothing to the light from the windows. This was her process to determine whether the clothes could be consigned or not. Any spot would mean it would go to charity. This job included all rooms of catalogued items and took the next two days. My tolerance for that activity in the past would have been totally zero…everything to charity, let's go home! But I'm older and less flappable or at least I accepted that I was captive and needed to conserve my emotional energy. We sorted the boxes, clothes and items throughout the house. I threw out all the makeup and personal items in the bathroom. We stopped briefly to enjoy the large and colorful matching plastic jewelry from the 1960s. Marian, was a colorful and actually very well-dressed person. We didn't get sad. We just did our job. We set aside the fine jewelry for relatives. Saturday night Dad took us to dinner in Pinehurst at a "$20 million renovation" of the hotel there and showed us all around the country club to see the "magnificent" preparations and expense taken to prepare for the U.S. Open, which was just a couple of weeks away. There was great irony in enjoying life at a nice dinner after sorting through the material goods of a dead person. My sister and I are both widowed and my Dad is a widower for the second time. We're tired of doing this. But life is sweeter and scarier because we know it is short. The three of us savored every morsel of food at dinner. Dad mused about how he would deal with seeing both wives in heaven…how that all works. Nancy and I looked at each other and sighed.

After we packed my sister's van with all of the consignable items, we headed home to Virginia. That was Monday. Dad said he would be up for the inurnment of Marian's ashes scheduled for thirteen days hence. My sister said he should stay with me, as she doesn't have the room with her son home for the summer. He said the day after the inurnment of her ashes at Arlington National Cemetery he was going to fly on the historic WWII B-17 somewhere in upper Maryland.

Anyway, Tuesday I was wiped out from the weekend and particularly irritable at work. Wednesday I came home and I heard a knock at the front door. When I opened the door, there stood my father, my dear old dad, with three suitcases, three hanging bags and a small box. With a sheepish but sad look he says to me, "Where do I put Marian?"

I gasp, and realize that the box is a first priority. I say "Up and away from the animals (my dog and cat)" thinking of the horror if they...

Marian (her ashes anyway) ended up on the top shelf of my front closet, just to the right of the 1945 mink that belonged to my mother, which I have never consigned. Close the closet door; forget both of them are in there. Dad moves in...for how long? Dunno.

Seven days later, my uncle and aunt from Charlottesville call to see if they can come on Tuesday to stay with me, even though the inurnment isn't until Friday. They probably wouldn't leave until Saturday...isn't that okay? Hmmm, that'll be 11 days of Dad and, now, my aunt and uncle for five days *all at the same time*. And my boyfriend trying to fit in somewhere along the way. He lives a mile away. I wondered if they could go there. Yeah, we could just switch!

Nope, just live with the wonders of the late seventies, early eighties (I mean their ages). For example, things like calling me at work when not one of the three of them could figure out how to run the dishwasher. (I deliberately didn't call them back for four hours, as I was sure they had figured it out. They all had dishwashers at home!) When I called back they said, "No, we were waiting for you to tell us".

I said, "Just shut the door, it starts" (*.>@!l&".llll!!!!). This was only the beginning. My aunt was determined to make me a meal, so one long evening was spent enduring the comments from all three of them about 1) my unsharpened knives ("You've got butter knives, not *real* knives"), 2) "Don't you know your light is out over the stove?" and, 3) "Your aunt is in horrible pain." She had just had back surgery seven days before. Such martyrs. I knew my offer to help, fix, save, rescue were not going to be heard. So I just sat on my couch and suffered. Dad was commenting on the "*#@@&!*#@("minority surgeon on a TV series. We all sat down to a wonderful dinner that I could barely enjoy, watching my aunt's pain, mostly self-inflicted by working so hard. Martyrdom is a strong familial trait in my family. I should know, I was being one myself.

Anyway, I worked late some nights. That helped. I love them but...

The mattress was too hard for one of them. I was proud of myself because I just let them work it out between them: They switched items, bedrooms and sheets all by themselves. And the three of them had to share a bathroom. I didn't give up my own room and private bath. I knew I needed to keep my sanity. I'm very proud of my ability to not martyr <u>all</u> the time. I think that is a real sign of growth!

My dog, cat and I were exhausted, trapped and pressured. I was the only one of us who felt guilty, because I am the human. I still had to work and had little quality time with them (the ol' folks).

Last November, my friend and I bought my dad a Muppets "Cookie Monster" because that is my dad's nickname and because Jim Henson was my dad's friend and co-worker in the early fifties (decade). The stuffed thing has a cookie on a ribbon around it's neck and it is all blue and when you put the cookie in his mouth (the toy, silly) it says three things while moving his arms in happy circles: "MMmmm, me hungry!" "Me *love* cookie, munch, munch, munch" and "munch, munch, munch" sounds. My Dad carries this with him wherever he goes. He puts it in the middle of the back seat of his Buick Le Sabre and puts a seat belt around him. On this same trip he brought him out to my sister's picnic table under his coat but only after he made a place setting for him. Actually, my dad hasn't gone totally senile; this is the child in him that he has displayed in the past. Just a fun lil' thing that gets a few laughs. And, I think he is comforted by the lil' guy lately.

I'm trying to figure out how I can prepare for my older years if I have the courage to live them: I guess I'll just write this stuff down and read it later. You say you'll never be like your parents...

After the inurnment, my dad packed up all of his things and left for the 3-17 flight. He said that he would head back home to North Carolina after that. Monday, my sister calls and says, "He's baacck!"

Twenty minutes later he leaves a voicemail at my work: "I just can't go home to the empty house again. Can I stay with you starting Wednesday?"

AAAAGGGGHHhhhhhh! So I begin to pace the office. I'm already nuts after two weeks of "company". *How* can I tell my own grieving father that he can't come stay with me and that I'm going *insane*?!! Also I had just found out that my aunt and uncle were coming back in three days to stay with me for their other niece's wedding. Three more days!? I called my deacon, my pastor, my friend, and talked it over with folks in the office. Everyone was very sympathetic, but no one provided advice. I decided to try telling Dad the *truth*: 1) I wasn't sure he would go home, 2) I thought I'd be "enabling" him not to deal with the grief and 3) I would be leaving for my sanity this weekend as others were returning as well...

I told him I was totally stressed out and that I would come see him for a weekend this summer and that he needed to go home and deal with things. The good news was that he didn't cry, get mad or hang up on me. He actually understood and said I was right. What a *grown* up Cookie Monster response!

I did leave the house to my aunt and uncle that weekend, before they even arrived. My uncle apparently had brought his knife sharpener, as upon my return there was a note lying next to all my newly-sharpened knives. The note said the deed was done and it was his pleasure. My only preparation for their visit was to fix the light over the stove and put out some towels. I was *outtathere*!   Perhaps I had overreacted but this was the first time I felt the potential role reversal.

Guess what? I just got a phone message from my aunt and uncle asking, "Can we please come up again next week for just *one* night so your Aunt Sarah can see her old Bridge playing friends?"

What would *you* do???????????????????????????????

Thanks for the lodgings. Had a big family get together and married off another young'un. — Awful lot of Browns lumped together. Missed the ... but didn't ... gorgeous.

BEWARE OF SHARPER KNIVES !

½ hr miscalculation was absolutely ... t did

Blessed Bellbottoms and the Great Cover-Up

1968

I believe that bellbottom pants were invented by God just for me. Perfect timing. This pants rage started about a year ago. When they first arrived, it was no big deal. I tried on several pair, very hopeful but they weren't quite wide enough to cover the brace. I tried on a pair of nice wool ones and various other materials without any luck. I stifle some tears as I try on each pair, but no luck. The bottom part of the pants just lies on top of the brace shoe. If I try to pull it down over the shoe it looks ridiculous, making the bottom of the pant leg into a stretched square. Pretty soon I could tell which ones wouldn't fit by looking at the selection on the rack. Finally, sometime this year, I saw what looked to be a perfect pair made of denim. What I saw when I put them on was incredible. I looked like a whole person. Even I could get by with these. Unless someone was really looking, you couldn't tell that my foot and leg are screwed up. I was overjoyed. Now if I can just work on not limping. The first time I wore them to a party I felt magnificent, poised and self-confident. Only I couldn't sit down as the pants would pull up to show the bottom portion of the brace. My good guy friends told me they thought I looked terrific without referring to the "cover up". They began to dance with me both fast and slow. They told me what a great dancer I am. I always wanted to be a dancer. They are very sweet young men. I'm lucky.

I have begun to wear more revealing clothes: hip-hugger bellbottoms in red, white and blue stripes and mid-riff blouses. When I wear both together my middle section is naked complete with belly button. Now with my long hair I feel as though I have become or am becoming a true hippie. Dad is already commenting on my shameless mini-skirts, he just hates flower children and makes foul comments on the breed daily. Too bad I have to wear skirts to school and church.

Saga in PA

1996

My sister-in-law, Kathy, was getting married on December 1, at her home in Pennsylvania. Kathy is a lawyer marrying a lawyer. She is only a little older than me, so marrying late in life.

I decided to take a train to Philly for the wedding as a less stressful way to get there. I could even sleep enroute. Jim had been dead a little over two years and, though I love them dearly, I hadn't seen much of his family.

The train left from Alexandria, Virginia, on time. It was very, very wet and cold outside so the train seemed charming and cozy once I was seated. I would need to change trains at the downtown Philly station but that was three hours away. I read and relaxed to the familiar clickety-clack of the train. I tried to remember what it was like going by train to Georgia as a little girl with my sister and Mom. I could remember the sleeper with its small sink and fold-down bed that was prepared by the steward at night. The nice man would knock on our door after dinner and say, "Misses Stuart? I'll make your bed now, if that's okay." Well, this train was just a comfortable chair with no one beside me. I was fine, content. The view out the window surprised me. It was very ugly. The view was the back of every warehouse through every dark side of each town along the way. Only occasionally on this route would we pass through small forests of pine trees and over lakes or rivers.

Despite the view, it was great to be traveling this way. The three hours seemed to pass too quickly. I really had to focus to come out of my daze and gather my things to get off at the Philly station. When I got off the train, I found a pay phone on the platform and called Liz, my other sister-in-law, to find out which stop to get off out her way. She told me St. David's. I looked around and marveled at the Bogie-esque scene: Gray city, dark train-depot shapes, smoky breath, steam coming out from trains as they hissed a minute while riders boarded, pigeons foraging through strewn and blowing trash and me leaning on a light pole. I even had on my London Fog raincoat. Wow, I thought, This is really neat.

The train to St. David's wasn't arriving for another ten minutes, so I had time to call my voicemail. I found out that my Aunt Boots had died. She had Alzheimer's for quite some time. I figured I could make it to the viewing the evening of my return. I called my erstwhile French fling in South America. The person who answered couldn't understand English, so I hung up. I just felt like I wanted to share the moment with him. This was *definitely* a Bogie movie scene.

As the train approached, the weather worsened. It was now spitting snow along with the sleet. It would only be a twenty-minute ride to St. David's. I boarded the train, located my seat, and lifted my rolling bag onto an open shelf above the seat. At that instant I heard a loud *crack* and knew that the combination of cold and weight of the bag caused my brace to bust a rivet. The brace was twenty years old. I had recently paid two hundred dollars to have a new one made, but it caused me to list too much to the left so I hadn't worn it. The aluminum one I was wearing had been extremely durable, with only one repair in 1980. It busted at work and a nice fellow from facilities took it to his friend while I sat trapped at my desk for a couple of hours. But this was going to be a challenge...out of town...wedding. Ugh.

Liz greeted me in the nasty drizzle at St. David's near her work, and I hobbled to her car explaining my dilemma. Mostly it wasn't destroyed but making a horrible amount of noise. We proceeded to a get a quick lunch at a nearby café, both of us laughing at the sound of the thing. A horrible squeaking emanated from it with each step. We strategized what to do about the brace during lunch after catching up on each other's families. When we arrived at her house in Berwyn, I perused her phone book for orthopedic places. The closest one had closed at one o'clock. So I suggested we try the nearest hardware store to buy a soldering iron which I knew would only be a stopgap. At least it could stop the noise (I could picture me coming into the church for the wedding. Not.)

Of course the more walking I did the worse the sound so by the time we arrived at the hardware store, there was a cacophony of sound emanating from the thing! We told a very nice gentleman the situation and he brought us a couple models of soldering irons. He said he thought I'd be wasting my money and that we should go to Devon Automotive a few miles down the road. He also said the town of Devon has the only welder he knows in the area and should be able to help me. We said we were willing to try it, so he gave us directions down a few back alleys to find the place. When we located the building it looked like a building that had been a stable but had been converted into a garage. I hobbled and squeaked toward the door, holding onto Liz.

The guy that came to the front was absolutely huge. He looked like an old-time blacksmith. I felt very vulnerable in this condition as I faced him. He looked at me quizzically. I told him why we had sought his help. I was here from Washington...for a wedding...can't wait until Monday...dead-in-the-water desperate. He said that since my brace was aluminum it wouldn't take a weld but that he could try a rivet. So we entered further into this very dark and creepy place. Within a few minutes he had fixed it, correcting the noise and making me safe to walk the streets of Pennsylvania. Although I was willing to pay him a hundred dollars for the deed, he said, "No charge."

We thanked him a whole lot and I whispered to Liz, as we walked out the door, "There really *is* a God."

Dr.'s Office: Lost and Found

2001

For the second time in several months I went back to find Dr. Weber's house. It had not occurred to me prior to this spring to ever go find the house. Why was I feeling the need to find the house? The memories were painful. (I had not seen it nor desired to find it. The last time I'd been to that office I was probably ten or twelve, almost forty years had passed.) But my sister had finally remembered the name of the street. She had told me but I had forgotten. I was sure that if my friend and I drove around enough I would remember what she told me.

We drove slowly for blocks through the beautiful old, wooded neighborhood with large trees that met high overtop of the little streets. We were beginning to give up as none of the street names sounded right. We decided to stop and pull out a street map from the back of the car. As soon as I saw the name on the map I remembered it was the one Nancy could recall: Gilden Street. I had known I was in the right neighborhood as many of the houses had deep brick-walled driveways. The only thing I could recall about the outside of the house was a door to the basement, the portal to the dreaded place, placed to the left of a walled-in driveway. But the houses I scanned as we drove up and down streets, only had narrow driveways with the deepening brick walls on each side. None had the door from there. Most had garages and were way too narrow. I could only recall (probably age ten or eleven when last there) that the driveway was wide enough for my mother to drive up, park and we could walk to the door. It had to be wider than a single car could traverse. I knew I could find it. But what if it was rebuilt, drastically changed? Why was I even *doing* this? I had to keep looking.

There were two parts to Gilden. When none of the houses had the door inside the driveway, I was relieved to see that Gilden continued on, a half block up where the other Gilden ended. The last house on the right had the door. I said, "That's got to be it." But, I wasn't sure. There was a woman working in the yard right next to the driveway. I asked my friend to turn the car around so I could get a better look. I was concerned whether the woman would be spooked by our scrutiny of her house. We pulled up just on the other side of the narrow street and my friend offered to get out and ask if the house had been the house of a doctor. Wild chance, I thought. It had been almost forty years. My friend got out and greeted the woman and then shouted to me, "Was his name Dr. Weber?"

We were at the right house. I couldn't believe it. I got out of the car and the woman said she had been living in the house for thirty-five years, and that Dr. Weber had been well known in the neighborhood. In fact, people in the area still call the house "Dr. Weber's house." She said Dr. Weber's son had stopped by not too long ago to see the house. That Dr. Weber moved to Arizona many, many years ago, and that a Dr. Smoot took over his practice, but was later murdered by a hit man in the middle of the night after a messy divorce.

She reminisced that her children played in the old exam rooms while they were growing up. I described my memory of the location of the waiting room, the nurse Belinda's office, the x-ray room, the narrow hall to the exam rooms one on the right and one on the left with Dr. Weber's office on the right in the middle of the little hall. She said it was exactly as I remembered it, she would give me a tour but that she had leased out the basement. I wanted to see it again but I didn't need to…it was very perfectly etched in my brain. The light green lacquered painted damp bumpy walls. The walls were textured like they had veins running through them. I remember running my fingers over the walls. I remember the dank carpet with wood blocks and other toys in the tiny waiting room. But most of all I remembered the squeak of the heavy door that entered that place. It first opened onto a teeny alcove. The door was dark and heavy. The door now had a white screen door and white inside door. She said she was sure it was the same door inside. It looked too much like a regular door to be the same door. The door I remember held power. Not only did you have to push hard to open it (air pressure) but it just screamed of the *doctor's* office. The smells. I know it would not have had the same smell, had I been able to enter. The door, the whole place seemed sad and harmless now. It has lost its power.

I'm not sure if I now feel a wave of missing my mother. After all, she was the "bad guy" taking me to that house of torture for so many years and so many shots. I mostly couldn't remember the place as I looked at it. It's like this wasn't the place at all. The sun was out. It was always dark and rainy when I came here as a child.

It reminds me that I am truly getting old. That it could be forty years since I was here seems implausible, but it was a real place, something in my life, part of who I am. After all there is no time. What is happening is still happening in some frozen zone of time. That's what I read in *Discover* magazine by a noted scientist.

My dog, Maggie was pulling hard to go in there. The woman, I asked her name, Jean, said that my dog might be smelling a cat.

I took several pictures. I'm not sure why I wanted to take pictures. I wanted to show them to my sister who shares similar painful memories. She could come here, too. It seems like a thousand miles away instead of fifteen miles from our houses. I told the woman that I was writing a book and that I had drawings from inside the office: one is of the exam room on the right and the empty exam table with a jar of lollipops on it. She seemed surprised by all that. She said her boys used to play with the wall buzzers and set things on the exam tables. It was a wonderful place for them to play. She said she had turned the x-ray room into a workroom but she still worries if it is safe!

I feel like someone died today. I'm not sure if it was me or if it was Mother. Something is different. I'm not sure what. As I traveled home on this beautiful, blue sky, white cloud summer day, I could remember what I felt as a child, feeling glad it was over as we started down Route 7. I tried to remember the car. I think the 1957 coral Pontiac. I tried to remember if I ever looked over at my mother in my misery. If I did, could I see how young and healthy she looked? How tired she must have been of dragging us to the doctors and listening to the whining there and back. Then I remembered going home and that I really wasn't happy back then. Life was very hard for a little girl like me.

But, maybe, I'm getting better all the time.

Post Mortem

1996

Two years since Jim died and living another day alone...and surviving. I can dance in my own house, dressed in sweats or naked, act like an idiot, cry like an idiot, call whoever I want to and not caring (much) about the cost. I can eat when I want to, sleep when I want to, disappear or travel when I want to. My calendar is highlighted for each social event, even the lunches or dinners with friends. Making a new life is weird and interesting work. Weird because I've never done it solo like this. I'm committed though to <u>never</u> commit to one person again. I want to fill my life with friends. No more death on my watch, please.

If I can have a healthy relationship without the debilitating commitment, there might be hope. Faith and hope shall keep me going. Just a little something to get through each day, thank you. And I go forward, continuing to walk sometimes with difficulty both in reality and cursing as I go, saying I love you to myself over and over out loud as I go. No one can know what this is like. Except for others that are afflicted.

My two husbands and friends were not interested in socializing so I didn't. Now I'm doing more than I ever have with a widening group of folks, friends. I have a chance to be the person I arrested in college when I left to get married. The writer, the artist, the social person that loves to be with people, energized by them. And that is *good* even when I got a lot of messages that it was *bad*! So here I am, God. Letting myself want like a human being, tired of being just a spiritual do-gooder. Ready to PAARRTTYY, thank you. Oh hell. Can I chop off twenty years, please?

Dopamine and Synapse

1965-Present

I did not have sexual intercourse until I was twenty and that was with my first husband. I have learned to appreciate a relationship with infrequent or no sex. I think that intellectual intimacy is more powerful. I had that bond with my late husband. Our synapses just synapsed, across a room, wordless, with a ton of chemistry thrown in. Our minds were melded. I have come close to that with another man. I treasure it and long for it when we aren't together. Honestly, the "in-love" part, the dopamine part that lasts about two years, is wonderful. But, it's always followed by noticing and loathing everything about the other person.

My life has been ritchly blessed with friends and lovers. I appreciate this more than any physically normal person can possibly imagine. Readers that are different in appearance know what I mean. The people that have come into my life - no matter how short the encounter - are very, very special people to me. They are, indeed, why I believe in the goodness of humans. They represent hope for the human race. They have overlooked my deformity to see me as a companion along the way. Even if the time we had was only a few hours, days or years, my feelings for them cannot be described. My feelings are strong and deep for every one of them. They are not friends or lovers, those are just words. They are the individual names, all equally important to me as they come into my moments. Beautiful in my eyes are they. Flawless even though flawed. I am filled with gratitude for their unconditional presence in my life. They are very great people, whether they succeed or fail in anything they do. The stories that follow give you only a glimpse into their very unique and individual characters. Each one holds a very special place deep in my heart and mind. I've told them all I love them. They can't know how deep that river flows...

Boys:
The Drummer

1965

I am almost fourteen, just finishing the eighth grade. I met him during one of those gatherings of the neighborhood boys and girls at my cousin's house. I watched him play the drums in his folk's basement and I desire him, even though I'm not sure what that means. I think he likes me because I have taken drum lessons. We take turns beating on the things like we know what we are doing. We have that in common anyway.

I received my first kiss from the Drummer while smashed into the back seat of a station wagon with my cousin and her boyfriend. They must have been used to kissing as they were ignoring the Drummer and I...all four of us laying butt to butt in the back of that small wagon. He is very nice looking and a small boy, with thin lips and nice teeth. His skin is olive. He has a German sounding last name. I'm not sure how we all ended up in the back of that car. It was parked in his folk's driveway. None of us are old enough to drive. We were just horsing around on a late spring Saturday evening when we ended up sitting on the tailgate of the wagon. This was the first time I felt the burning up sensation that comes with being turned on. I was absolutely afire with the closeness of his warm breath as I lay on my back and he breathed close into my neck, face and hair. And then after an eternity of heat radiation, he began placing small kisses on my right cheek. Soon after this, I turned toward him and accidentally got kissed square on the mouth. I think I wanted to run away, but the pounding in my chest made me deaf and immobile. He was so close to me that his long eyelashes were brushing my cheek with each blink. I was told later by a friend that these are called butterfly kisses. So much, so suddenly and it wasn't over. After a little while he stunned me when he pressed his silver ring into my hand and asked me to "go steady". I don't think I spoke, I just took the ring. I could picture it hanging proudly about my neck, a trophy of this first encounter. Popular girls at school could show they are worthy and "owned" by having some cheap ring hanging around their necks (green from the cheap chain).

Soon, I could hear my cousin's older brother yelling for us, his voice getting louder as he walked up the dark road. When he spotted us in the car he yelled, "What are you <u>doing</u>? All of you get home!" He wasn't much older but old enough to be in charge. I didn't care. I was floating somewhere above the trees. My first high: no drugs or alcohol.

I had been staying at my cousin's house for the weekend while my folks were away. Sunday night my uncle drove me to the neighbor's across the street from my house. My folks wouldn't be home until very late Sunday night so they had arranged for me to stay across the street at the Adams' house. Then I could ride to school Monday with their daughter. I had hardly slept Saturday night and was having an awful time settling down at the neighbor's. I was in a room facing my house and just couldn't stop thinking about what had happened to me. Soon I could see the headlights of my parents' car and watched them pull into our driveway. I thought I would just bust with the excitement I was feeling. I couldn't wait to tell them my wonderful news so I waited a little while for them to get settled. I then woke my neighbor lying in the other bed to tell her that my folks were now home and I would quietly leave.

The night air was cool and sweet as I walked quietly across the cul de sac and up the steep drive to my house. I purposely made enough noise coming in the front door so they wouldn't be startled. The house was dark and they were already upstairs. I timidly tapped on their door and opened it.

They were laying in the dark. I could only see their forms under covers by the hall light. I blurted, "Guess what? I'm going steady!"

There was a tremendous silence and then Mama said, "What?" in a breathy voice, trying to hide her shock. (Mama was so reserved I never really knew what she was feeling. I had never seen her cry.)

Daddy then said, "I don't want a daughter of mine getting pregnant before she's sixteen!"

Stunned by the statement and the sound of deep anger in his voice, I still managed to giggle, "No Daddy! You don't have to worry about THAT!" Did he mean to say it that way, like it would be *okay* to get pregnant at sixteen?

The statement stung me and I felt disappointed they weren't happy for me. All I had received were some sweet kisses and a silver ring all at the same time. It seemed pretty special to get kissed and a ring. I knew it could be a world record. I don't remember going to bed. The thrill was gone.

I became very ill for two weeks after that. Mama took me to a specialist for tests on my stomach. I even had x-rays. They didn't think it was an ulcer but perhaps a spastic colon. I ran a low-grade fever the entire time. I was invited to two parties and made it to one of them the second week but felt awful. And my Drummer was there. He totally ignored me. My cousin and one of her girlfriend's and I went to my cousin's house after the party for a sleepover.

My cousin and her friend snuck out the sliding doors of the rec room where we camped out. A couple of the boys had planned to come by outside for a while. I felt too sick to go out. In about an hour my cousin and her friend came back in and walked over to me and said, "He asked me to ask you for his ring back and to say he's sorry." I gave it to her. I didn't feel angry. I watched as she went back outside. I am a very young girl and don't feel too good. I don't know anything about sex, love or puppy love. But this certainly had been an interesting beginning…

Role in my life: He gave me hope of having a normal life. That a relatively attractive young boy could like and even KISS me was huge for me, a physically disfigured person.

One summer after eighth grade, my cousin introduced me to the Boy on the Bicycle. He stopped by her house one day while I was visiting her. She introduced me to him. His name is Neil something. She didn't mention his last name. He's a small guy with dirty blond hair and a big nose. He seems quiet but nice. He snickers when he laughs. I can't remember when I saw him next.

My dear, dear friend. He was homely and felt unloved. He had a great sense of humor and musical talent but that wasn't enough. He drove a Volkswagon bug with antlers sticking out of the top; went to military school for his junior and senior year because he was failing high school; later joined the navy medical corps, flipped out on drugs and killed himself. Some of his friends blamed me, including him, because I dumped him to marry my first husband (not really, I didn't even know that Neil cared until after I started dating my future husband. Some defense). I wrote a eulogy to him after he died and had about a hundred pamphlets printed for his family and friends. I didn't find out he died until two weeks after the funeral. This is too painful to write about…

Role in my life: He helped me get through my difficult teenage years and we totally bonded on music, laughing, talking and friendship. We needed each other unbelievably at that time. He was my first gift.

And then there was the somewhat platonic friend that got a scholarship to get his masters degree at Yale, studied at the Louvre, later became a professor at Princeton, and is now a curator at the Smithsonian.

Role in my life: He was the first to intellectualize me.

The Frenchman was my first real date in high school. Only one other boy actually asked me out on a date. The other relationships developed from just "hanging out". We saw a very bad movie. I met him through my cousin at a party. He was two years my senior. I fought him off on every date, from age fifteen through seventeen. My mother wanted me to marry him. He was French. My mother spoke and taught French (Georgia style). His parents met in the French underground. His father was in the diplomatic corps. Years later, he introduced me like I was his big sister to both of his future wives. His first wife still works in the government, the second is the mother of his two children. I haven't met the recent third. I followed him off to college like he was my brother, and he fought with me like one. My parents were relieved to know that was driving off to Kansas City for college with him for my first years away. Little did they know that he was an absolute sex fiend.

Years later, in a brief phone call I was sharing my worries with him about not having a job with medical benefits for my two small children. In passing, he suggested I contact a company he had heard of that had great people and benefits. I got a job on a walk-in and have been employed there for twenty-four years.

Role in my life: He was my Clark Gable friend who sucked the air out of a room with his charm and beauty and made me feel desirable during some of

my worst, most undesirable, moments…and his casual recommendation
launched my long career.

Then there was SYIAM. That wasn't his name. That was how we
ended up signing the hundreds of letters we sent back and forth when he was in
college. It stood for See You In a Minute. This friend was so smart he went
away to college at sixteen, following his older brother to the same mid-west
college I would attend in a couple years. His mother was a senior official in a
U.S. government agency, and they lived in Udorn, Thailand for a while. He sent
me earrings from there. I lost one and put the other on a charm bracelet. His
father died of cancer when he was very young. I had met him about the same
time as the Drummer, the Boy on the Bike, the Monk and the Frenchman.

Role in my Life: SYIAM's letters got me up on days while I was waiting
for a social life. I would thrill at the sound of the mail coming through the slot
in the front door and see his scrawl on an envelope lying on the floor. I saved
every letter but I think my first husband threw them out after we separated.
SYIAM and I still keep in touch by email now. He is married with a daughter in
the midwest.

Also during my high school years there was the fabulous and brilliant
Cuban artist. He graduated from high school the same year he graduated from a
well-known university in Washington, D.C.,…at age seventeen. He, his parents
and brother had come to the United States on a grant from a foundation for his
exceptional art talents. I met him in "home room" in eleventh grade. On
weekends we would walk around the streets of Washington while I was
attending art classes in the summer. He and I once visited Dumbarton Oaks in
Georgetown and pretended we were in the movie "Blow-Up". I went to his
studio and his first art show in Georgetown. Once we walked from my house to
a lake to swim (I just watched). He compared me to Kafka and Gibran in a
weird note in my high school yearbook. When at the art school, he would dress
well. I specifically remember how he looked in a white suit and pink shirt. He
was tall, lanky and quite handsome except for a few crooked teeth. Perhaps that
is why he would spend time with me. He understood but ignored this single
flaw in himself. He was a bit odd in other ways. After all, he was an artist.
He welded mylar into large clear brown empty cubes.

In the 1970s, a friend brought to my attention a story about the Cuban
artist on the front page of the "Style" section in the *Washington Post*. He was
making the scene in New York as part of something called the "hyper trendy
set." He owned a combination gallery and bookstore there. Later, in 1989, my
intellectual friend came to my door holding out a popular magazine. The cover
displayed a picture of my Cuban friend with his beautiful wife. The article
described his "high class" life, rich friends, brief and bankrupt business
designing men's shirts, many personalities, his South American wife of royalty,
the second largest diamond ring in the world that he gave her, their child and his

recent imprisonment in Italy for allegedly embezzling millions of dollars. He had been a pal of Picasso and his wife, and a famous writer wrote about him. Sad about his situation, I wrote to the author of the article hoping to get word to him that I was sorry things were such a mess. At seventeen, he was enamored with Marlene Dietrich, about eighty years old at the time, and he would play her records over and over. I understood from the book written about him that he hired her lawyer to represent him.

Role in my life: He opened the rest of the door to art for me, introduced me to a well-known art school and gallery where I became employed for four summers. His brief role in my life, helped begin the baby steps that would help lead to my career ten years later.

Another great friend earned degrees in literature and range sciences from universities out west. He studied mime in Paris under Marcelle Marceau, worked briefly at my company as a land reclamationist, herded cows in Montana, worked in a tobacco shop, taught ESL and taught life boat at a Merchant Marine School, found God and is now a Monk (he used to be Presbyterian, then Episcopal, then Catholic but he had been married several years while in Montana and would need an annulment to become a priest. Besides, he was too old). We have a lot of spiritual discussions and he is a dear life-long friend that calls or visits about once a year when visiting his sister.

Role in my Life: He took me to my senior prom in fake sideburns, his father's tux and his own tennis shoes and ordered me Guinness Stout beer, which I hated, at a fancy Washington restaurant. More importantly, he held my left hand while another friend held my right in the hospital waiting room while my son lay critically ill, and we thought dying, in 1984.

{Isn't this all incredibly unbelievable to read about? All true, I tell you. Who woulda thought that "the little, crippled girl" as my high school art teacher described me, could have such a bizarre life. Or doesn't that seem absolutely appropriate, believable? Bizarre for the bizarre, hmmmm.}

College Guys

1969

The first few dates at college were just okay. But one of them began in October and lasted through the entire first year. Incredibly, this one, the Singer, came back into my life, twenty-five years and two lifetimes later.

We saw Peter, Paul and Mary on our first date. He persuaded this guy from across the hall to drive us but only after we got him a date, my roommate. (The driver became my first husband two years later). Anyway, the Singer and I fell so hard in love that we both abandoned all others. He would sing his own tunes and country songs for the campus with great reviews. For some reason this singer and jock (my first jock!), who attended college on a swimming scholarship, courted me royally. It ended slowly the next summer. We had gotten too serious. I was furious for a while after returning to school, and being dumped, but soon developed a relationship with his new roommate, the sports editor.

I had become editor-in-chief of my college newspaper, which helped keep my mind off my hurt. My new friend had been selected as the sports editor of the paper, so we spent a lot of time together. We had dinner once a week on the day the newspaper was stuffed into campus mailboxes. I couldn't handle the criticism, real or imagined. It was uncomfortable to watch the faces of the students as they were reading the paper at dinner in the Commons so I learned to hide off-campus and he would accompany me. We also made regular trips to UMKC's library and parked at Swope Park for the occasional "kissy face" and fruit-flavored Right Time beer. He would drive me to the *Kansas City Star* where I worked to get three credit hours. Anyway, he had a girl back home, who coincidentally, had my first name. He was reportedly devastated when I left school to marry my first husband but I thought they must have been talking about his girlfriend from home because we had the same first name. My husband-to-be dropped out the year before and joined the army as a journalist. He was stationed at Arlington Hall in Virginia before he was assigned to Asmara, Africa; at the last moment, the army changed the assignment to Hawaii of all places!

I didn't even *need* to get married! But I liked the farm boy from Illinois with his toe head and love for children. My first recollection of him, even before I dated the Singer is sketched by me in a scrapbook: the way I first saw him...leaning against a pillar in a dorm lobby with his head down, sad and lonely. I was a total sucker for that. Later he was the father of my two children. He is now remarried and lives in San Francisco.

Role in my life: Father of my children. I will be forever grateful. And wonderful years in Hawaii...

The Sports Editor, Role in my life: He was such a good friend that we often felt connected even when apart. He would call me at my dorm and ask if I was okay when he just "knew" I wasn't. Years later he called me to discuss his decision about marrying a Catholic girl. He did. He teaches swimming at a Missouri high school and they have two children. When trying to select a middle name for my newborn son, I decided my sports editor's first name was the right one. My husband liked it, too.

Another very good college friend, who was an associate editor on the paper, called to me when seeing me from behind while I walked across campus, "Hey, step-and-a-half!" Because I knew his voice, I wasn't wounded. But prior to this moment, very few spoke of "it," my very obvious physical flaw, and only fewer ever shouted about it. But this friend was accurate. There it was, what I wanted no one to see. What he called out to me. It was me.

Post Mortem

1998

An important relationship after my husband died was with my first boy friend in college, the singer-swimmer. We reconnected after twenty-five years. He never married. He'd recently moved cross-country to be near me and then got a good job, but I have not yet made a commitment. I feel mean.

Role in my Life: He helped me through one of the toughest times of my life, the death and grieving of my second husband, by planning beautiful journeys: a cruise, trips through the Southwest and lots of caring and calling and support even when I became pretty abusive in my grief.

I dated a few others after Jim died, men I had met while traveling. One was a few years younger than me, the other ten years younger, the other four years older. Each added as a life-long friend and good company. I wondered about the one that asked me on a date to a Chargers game in San Diego. He drove from LA and I flew from DC for our date. But he became interested in someone else. I'm invited to their wedding this summer.

Role in my life: Normalcy! Lots of space. No strings. Good friends.

I'm fighting fiercely to keep my independence, my space, especially after losing my one true love to cancer. Meanwhile, I pace the house trying to think what life is going to bring me next or what I should seek or how it is all going to come out before the reaper comes for me. I figure my life has been pretty darn strange with some hard stuff and tons to celebrate.

Rejection

1955 to Present

When you are a blight, or feel like you are, or really are, people do stare, gawk, guffaw...you never really forget it. It just manifests itself in hypersensitivity to every other thing that "doesn't feel so good". But only occasionally does somebody say something cruel (although anybody tacky enough to ask me personal physical questions in public, I have thought cruel and insensitive).

Well, I wanted to get my license (I was sixteen) and I went to this old house in Falls Church (really the DMV) and asked a man for the application for a learner's permit. He looked at my physical self and LAUGHED (guffawed!) and said, "You're kidding!? You can't drive with that thing."

I said, "Oh yes I can".

And he said, "Well, I guess you could drive an automatic, but you'll need a doctor's letter stating that." He gave me the form and I, again, felt scarred. You see, I don't see myself the way the world does. I didn't get my license until four years later when I was about to be married.

But of course, I overreacted. Right?

A&P grocery store, hometown: My earliest memory, age four or five, when the world started telling me I was different. Come in store entrance with Mama, get cart, stop. Woman asks Mama what's wrong with your little girl?

College, Red X, buying beer with friends: Two guys follow me through the store and say for many to hear but directed to me: "At least you've got one pretty leg". He said it with a sneer. Even my friends were outraged.

Washington, D.C., lunch hour on summer job: While crossing Pennsylvania Avenue at intersection at 17th Street, I fall. Someone makes ugly remark. I give them the finger.

Boston, Children's Hospital: During examination to explore possibility of amputation. I'm wearing my feminine pad and lying undressed on the exam table and the doctor calls in my parents to discuss my case. X-ray of my hands and every part. Hours. Mortified. Sobs.

Playground: Boys mean to me. I threaten to hit them where it hurts with my brace.

Playground: Kick ball and softball. Someone always runs the bases fo me. Nice but it feels like pity.

Grass and brick: Can't walk straight.

Malls, grocery stores, all stores, all streets, all parks, kids, all airports...all public places: Hate it.

Knock at the door of my townhouse in Illinois. Two women representing a religious group came in, showed me a passage in their book, and told me that my leg was caused by some sin of my parents or ancestors. I asked them to leave.

Recurring dream: Me naked in public places. Ashamed. No where to hide or cover up. Keep walking.

Questions, questions, questions.

Shoes: Buy one pair. Throw left one away. Put brand new unusable right shoes in a big box to give to a friend for his birthday. Yes, yes I pay full price.

Pants: Bellbottoms gone. No cover up. Hours of searching. Give up forever.

Handicap parking permit: thirty years old, I finally got one because women on my staff wanted to go to the mall at Christmas. Dirty looks. Have to show them when I get out. Sometimes they apologize.

Wanna hide.

Love to dance. Used to dance.

Can't check mail when it snows.

Son in wheelchair. No, no relationship.

Daughter is now asked questions by friends about me. The pain continues and is now shared. Wrong.

At a conference in Orlando, Florida, a corporate executive upon being introduced to me looks down and says only these words, "Why haven't you done anything about that?"

I finally made some progress at the airport in LA. I passed a long line of "starers" waiting to get on their plane. The line had about fifty of them in the middle of the walkway at one of the terminal gates. They were in a single file line waiting to board a plane. I intentionally let them know what they were doing wasn't going to go unnoticed. For the *very* first time, I leaned way down to where their eyes were and pointed my thumb up and said, "Eyes up, please!" I just was in a pissy mood and think it was way overdue. I've always wanted to do that. I felt cocky enough to do it three times to folks in that line. There were probably at least twenty that gave me the usual once over (sans my head!). It even made me smile pridefully as I strutted on by...

Hum

2001

Today was one of those dreamy spring days in Virginia. Every pink, white, yellow and purple thing has bloomed and is being nudged out of the way by the light, deer-nibbling green, leafy things. As I look up, every pastel color presents a painting against the deep blue background with light white cotton clouds moving slowly along in the breeze that caresses my skin. Too sweet I think. Is this why every life should ask, "Shall I live to see another spring?" It almost hurts it is so lovely. Not beautiful like the majestic mountains of Colorado or California or Hawaii, but subtle and light...only sickening sweet because it is so fleeting here. I can only feel this way coming out of a long winter of dark grays, dreary cold with stick trees and huddling against the biting wind. It's like after you have the flu and the first taste of a banana or dry toast or cool water when you feel better.

There is a much kinder wind today. We call it a breeeeeze I think because that word only begins to describe what it feels and looks like when it is moving the things that are shining in the sun like a blade of grass or the light golden outer strands of my dog, Maggie's red coat. She even fell into a drowsy sleep driving back after we celebrated the day by watching boats on the lake at Fountainhead Park. And the birds could even be heard over the traffic on our return: chirping, tweeting, clucking, and singing!

I stopped for a sandwich in a small place near Occoquan. I couldn't understand why I suddenly felt so relaxed at noon on a day after a hectic week at work. The humming of the coke machine was soon determined the cause. That rhythmic noise in the background was unbelievably soothing and I wondered why it was so familiar. It led me directly toward pleasant childhood memories of falling asleep on a brutally hot, humid night in my bedroom with the back-and-forth little black fan with the rusty blades at the foot of my bed. Back...pause, whirr...and forth...pause, whirr. The dreamy day and the pleasant hum reminded me of those few seconds when that small fan on the floor would blow blessed air on my sweaty little body as it passed. It had a big silver metal switch that I was scared to flip because I had been warned of the danger of the spinning blades.

Which led me to another sound. Although my parents never got central air conditioning until long after I left home, they did have a small window air conditioner painted pink to match their bedroom walls. I would go close the door of that room, lie down on their bed, smelling of mud-pie making, salty dirt and fell asleep to that wonderful humming sound and cool air that soon caused me to bring the bedspread backward over part of me and take an un-enforced nap!

Which led me to even more sounds from my past; of the big window fan we bought for the kitchen, which was a very big deal. It was placed in the window just over the tiny kitchen table. I was amazed at its big size, function and noise. I could actually turn the button on top to make it pull hot air out of the kitchen and then speed it up or slow it down. I would be scolded if I made the fan blow air IN because it blew everything around in the kitchen. My favorite thing was to talk right into it so I could hear the blades mincing my voice into little fast pieces. I remember doing this once just before one of my birthday parties when it was about one-hundred degrees and I got sick and had to send everybody home. And that memory led me to the soothing sound of the little refrigerator in the kitchen with the handle that pulls out to open it. It was a big deal to turn it off and defrost it with a table knife and bucket.

Just down the two steps from the kitchen I can remember the sound of the milkman picking up the milk bottles out of the metal milk box by the door…clink, clink and putting in new ones...clunk, clunk. Mama would sometimes put a note in the milk box to order cottage cheese and buttermilk to go with her cornbread she made. He was the Sealtest man in a white truck with a white hat. One day the milk box was gone and we never saw him again. But THAT led to the summer sound of the clanging bells of the Good Humor truck and panicky call to Mama for money so I can run-hobble across the front grass to get my purple double Popsicle before he moved on….

More summer sounds at my aunt and uncle's beach cottage, Franella. It was named for my uncle's grandparents, Frank and wife, Ella. We cousins would sleep on the wooden cots on the front screened in porch and I would snooze at mid-afternoon or late evening barely noticing the squeaking open and flap shut of the screen front door and bare feet treading across the wood floor. And that brings the smell of fishy salty air and the sounds of the motor boats in the distance somewhat muffled by the hot air as the noise filters over a short time to my sleepy ears.

On Saturday afternoons, I recall the sound of the lawn mower. There were two kinds. One was the type without a motor that I remember sitting idle most of the time. The other was very loud to include my father's cursing when he would pull and pull on the handle but it would sputter and not start. And then another child's nap with the open window and the sound of the lawn mower going away and coming back as I snoozed again…

While all this beauty and musing is nice, I never have felt settled in Virginia. My heart and mind holds other places even more dear with their own sounds and memories.

Bricks, Cobblestones, Slate and Gravel,
A Pain In My Ass!!

2001

It seems to be getting worse. Nice, smooth pavement, blacktop, asphalt, vinyl, linoleum and carpet are being replaced by brick. Beautiful brick. Masonry on the floor. It's inside of buildings, airports, entryways. It's in the street, on the sidewalks, on paths from here to there. It's in steps at metro and railway stations and subways. It's at the harbors, in museums. Beautiful brick.

Sometimes short cobblestones are added for classic beauty. A lovely mix of beautiful brick and cobblestone. Like between the boardwalk and the pier at Hermosa Beach (*swear*).

Where there is no brick there is slate, all wavy and bumpy and in my way...

All bloody roadblocks for me. Bricks and cobblestones are really not as bad as gravel or grass. But they are more insidious as you can't tell until you get closer to determine the degree of threat of the obstacle. It would be good to know ahead of time. As my husband would whisper to me, "Brick alert!", we would steel ourselves and hang on to get there (if only he had a "normal" wife). If we could see it was a long stretch of uneven terrain, we would get in the car and try to find a handicapped parking spot though that can be a challenge. Sometimes we abandoned a good time to avoid the strain!

It depends on how the brick and mortar are laid. Sometimes the mortar is laid high between the bricks so there is only a little bit of unevenness. But normal brick or aging brick is a death trap (well, almost!)

Pushing my son in a wheelchair across gravel or grass, well that is a site to see! I'm old enough to swear aloud and not care if I am heard. My son is still too polite. And he is heading to Poland as I write...on Air France. They treat crips like crap. But that's another story.

Anyway, the toll on my lower back is settling in as I age...as I teeter across the landmines lain prettily before me. Others don't seem to understand what it's like to have a stilt to balance on. Usually I just go down on my ass and/or my hand and/or my knee or just all of the above. But not if I am very, very careful. But then I look like an ass.

I hate asking for help or a hand or an arm. So I don't. So sometimes I go down. Oh, lovely, lovely brick and cobblestones. And gravel is so cheap that it's almost everywhere! I used to avoid going to my son's T-ball practice and games. First I had to cross gravel then a mile of grass to get to the seats. "I'll just stay in the car and watch, honey." But that was only a few years before his illness and he would be dealing with this himself.

Grass is pretty and I believe we need to stop scabbing over the earth with anything non-earthy...but *please* just give me a straight white ribbon of hard sidewalk from "a" to "b" and while you're at it, through the woods and somehow to the beach (could you roll it up at night?) to make me gleeful and stop the swearing!!

And by the way, please stop laying uneven planks of wood on the floor. It just looks really great. Stop it!!

But as one friend observed, it's not practical to go to the expense for a minority! True.

Whine....

My Beloved Portofino

2000

January

Really bad migraine today. After three Excedrin and two Tylenol I went to park at the beach off the Esplanade in Redondo Beach and tried to focus on the waves instead of my head. Not too successful though I did note the Good Year blimp going by just off shore in the mist and the sailboats that seemed to be floating in mid-air on the horizon and the man sweeping up the parking lot in his filthy clothes that stopped to lean on the fence and gaze at the beach scene (not a bad job I thought) and the people heading down the steps to the beach with coffee and blankets as it is sixty degrees (hot compared to the blizzard back home).

Then my thoughts would move to scenes with Jim staring at the Chesapeake Bay from the Bronco in the morning. And how I would feel with him there.

I went back to the Portofino hotel. While walking the halls I tried to remember which oceanside room on which floor he and I stayed back in the Spring of 1984, sixteen years ago.   And I vividly remember the picture I have at home of him on the balcony of that room with the sailboat going by behind him. And I have been watching the sailboats go by each time I stay here, but he is gone.

Right now I am in the lobby of this beautiful special place and watching the sun lower, about five fingers above the jetty, just over darkening clouds. And the birds are flying peacefully hither and yon on this January day.

This pain is so exhausting. I need the light but my head hates it right now. I consider getting a facial later in hopes that it will soothe me. I feel old toda
Would Jim have still loved me as I age? He fell in love with me in my youth
He was my age when I met him. I can smell him right now. So clean and sweet…and untouchable. Even that night in 1984 when we went out to dinn
he was crisp, smartly casually dressed and beautiful.

That weekend we headed south and stopped in San Juan Capistrano
our way to San Diego. He, behind his dark sunglasses, quiet but totally *with*
We were soul mates. Is that why I can't love again? Will I ever truly love again?

And I need to lose the weight I have gained. I don't feel healthy an
hale like I did when I was walking.

There was a fellow this morning at Scotty's flirting with me across tables. Do you know what I said to him two tables away when he asked, "D
you promise to call me next time you are in town?"

I said very low, dreading his pitiful reaction when I would get up so he would see me for who I really am, "You won't say that when you see me get up." I don't know if he heard me but it took the usual courage to stand and walk away as the silence was deafening when I went in full view to the cashier knowing that he would feel awful about flirting with a cripple.

I still don't feel worthy of anything I have. God, help me with all of it and forgive my sins of self-absorption and the other things you know.

February

Magnificent day today. High seventies, deep blue sky and brilliant sunshine and a good first visit to the Getty Center with a dear friend. I had a wonderful time.

Just came into the Portofino after watching the sunset over the Pacific. What I noted: White seagull bellies half-bathed in a pink light from the sun a finger above the water. Birds clucking happily in the palm fronds. Surf spewing over the jetty with the foam cast in the same pink light. Seals bobbing up and down in the water. An older, beautifully-tanned California woman with her blonde hair pinned up and her gold edged sunglasses and white silk slacks and white high-heeled sandals puffing softly on her cigarette as she views the same scene.

And the intense sun is sinking from view leaving only an orange glow, hundreds of gulls still swooping and floating as they turn their heads left to right, cocked downward to find their supper. Lovely ending to a grand day. (I don't want to go home...)

Roomie

1969-Present

She played Blood, Sweat and Tears on our shared record player while roommates in a small college near Kansas City.

I was in her wedding when she was nineteen and saw her just before the demise of her first marriage. They had one boy. She married and divorced him again after having two more children.

Like me, she has had a long career with a large corporation. We have witnessed each other's lives by telephone ever since she left, thirty-two years ago. She had only been there four months.

Our telephone conversations have followed two themes: "Hi, I'm in pain" and "Hi, I'm in love again". We have cried and laughed and have been brutally honest with each other. She was on the other end of the line during my husband's illness. I was there just after she found out her daughter, at seventeen, was pregnant. And she called me after she received the news that her former husband had been found nearly dead in his apartment and was in a nursing home with brain damage from years of alcohol.

We giggled when she fell in love with a man that had rented a room in her basement. He was fifteen years younger.

We never remember each other's birthdays and rarely send Christmas cards. But she has been in Cincinnati, Atlanta or Orlando by telephone while I was in Hawaii, Illinois, Utah, Colorado, Virginia, Nebraska or California.

I hated listening to Blood, Sweat and Tears over and over and over in our small no-escape dorm room. When visiting her in Florida a few years ago, I took great joy when finding the dreaded album near her stereo, and wickedly played it full blast to wake her at o-dark-thirty, in her bedroom on the other side of her beautiful Florida home. Pay back.

As much as I hate to say (sing) it: "You made me so very happy. I'm so glad you came into my life."

Salon

2001

I was receiving a facial in California. I asked the technician where she was from and she said Brazil. While receiving the layers of moisturizers and aromatherapy we talked about our lives and the men in our lives in general. She said she felt unbelievable guilt about leaving her country and her family. She had left to get away from the shame of a broken engagement. Her dad later died there without her helping. Then she had an abortion. She can't forgive herself for any of it. She recently had a dream about her baby boy as a man all in white on a swing with a woman and very happy. Her father owned an orange plantation. When the technician was a little girl her mother peeled oranges so that they fell on the ground. The orange peels formed letters…four of them. Each letter was the first initial of the men that came later in her life. She can't explain that. They come and go in her life she says. They either die or leave. I told her I understood.

They were very nice to me in that salon. They wanted to hear about my book and my life and my family. The owner took me to my car so I wouldn't mess up my nails. She unlocked it and put the key in the ignition.

Motherhood

2001

Letter to my kids, Peter and Sarah: Mother's Day, 2001

Dianne, my college roomie, sent me the text next to the arrows below, last week just a couple days before she became a grandma again. I cut it down and inserted my "relational" memories of both of you…:

> *This is for all the mothers who have sat up all night with sick toddlers and who walk around the house all night with their babies when they keep crying and won't stop.*

Of course you both would plant your hot, feverish feet on my back in the middle of the night. You would breath rapidly, be a little "crazy" but always in good humor. (The colic wasn't so funny however!) I'd do it again in a second, and just hold you even tighter!

> *This is for all the mothers who show up at work with spit-up in their hair and milk stains on their blouses and diapers in their purse.*

I remember this pretty well. Sort of that sour smell that clings to your clothes but no time to change before you run out the door! Markings of a mom… (Yep and I had those nice little folded diapers in my purse but I thankfully didn't have to work outside the home while you were babies!)

> *For all the mothers who run carpools and make cookies and sew Halloween costumes. And all the mothers who DON'T.*

The last line is my favorite, of course. You would both giggle (and still do) when I would attempt to cook or bake anything! Toast, boiling water, etc. I wanted to do it "right" but eventually I, and you, had to accept me for who I am. It's amazing you survived at all! Boxed macaroni and cheese for my little ones that sat on their knees and rocked the chair forward and backward while using fingers to stuff hard, little uncooked noodles in their mouths! (Thanks for forgiving me this one. At least your dad was a chef!) And of course, my love for you and the outrage at myself finally put me back behind the wheel so we could go to and fro together. Sorry about not being the car-pool Mom though. We got to know a few cab drivers, didn't we!? And, yes, I did get a "D" in high school in sewing in home ec!

➢ *This is for the mothers who gave birth to babies they'll never see. And the mothers who took those babies and gave them homes.*

I can't even imagine the horror of this. And the courage. Thank God I never knew this part.

➢ *This is for all the mothers who froze their buns off on metal bleachers at football or soccer games Friday night instead of watching from cars, so that when their kids asked, "Did you see me?" they could say, "Of course, I wouldn't have missed it for the world," and mean it.*

Peter: T-ball and screaming, wildly competitive parents all around (now THAT was hard!). Sarah: Ballet. My artist. You were filled with joy and terror. Sorry I didn't keep taking you to lessons when you still wanted to go.

➢ *This is for all the mothers who yell at their kids in the grocery store and swat them in despair when they stomp their feet like a tired two-year old who wants ice cream before dinner.*

I remember this! We would all be nuts for a little while after leaving the store. Each of us being terribly human! Of course, we best remember the large yellow-boat car on the cross country trip when you both stood in the back corner of that huge car when I tried to swat at you in vain. My arms were too short!

➢ *This is for all the mothers who sat down with their children and explained all about making babies. And for all the mothers who wanted to but just couldn't.*

did this safely at an age when you couldn't remember and claimed I did it just like MY mother did! Do better than me with this, okay!?

➢ *For all the mothers who read "Goodnight, Moon" twice a night for a year. And then read it again. "Just one more time."*

Okay, another "flat spot" in mothering. I just couldn't sit still long enough! (I remember doing this SOME times!)

➢ *This is for all the mothers who taught their children to tie their shoelaces before they started school. And for all the mothers who opted for Velcro instead.*

did this and your Dad, too. I was amazed at how quickly both of you learned dress yourself. But I do remember that bib overalls were a challenge for both of us!

> *This is for all mothers whose heads turn automatically when a little voice calls "Mom?" in a crowd, even though they know their own offspring are at home.*

Every small voice is yours.

> *This is for all the mothers who sent their kids to school with stomachaches, assuring them they'd be just FINE once they got there, only to get calls from the school nurse an hour later asking them to please pick them up. Right away.*

SORRRYYY!

> *For all the mothers who bite their lips sometimes until they bleed - when their fourteen year olds dye their hair green.*

Sarah, I think was the red prom dress with the large rhinestones. Peter, it was the pig stealing incident your senior year.

> *What makes a good Mother anyway? Is it patience? Compassion? Broad hips? The ability to nurse a baby, cook dinner, and sew a button on a shirt, all at the same time? Or is it heart? Is it the ache you feel when you watch your son or daughter disappear down the street, walking to school alone for the very first time?*

Or out the door for their first date? Or down the center aisle to get their diplomas? Or onto the train going back to college for the umpteenth time, or up the street alone in a car to drive back to college? Or through the gate at the airport to go back to their adult homes? Or hanging up the phone on Mother's Day, while I am three thousand miles away in California? (Broad hips, is true however!)

> *The need to flee from wherever you are and hug your child when you hear news of a fire, a car accident, a child dying?*

Been there....done that!

> *For all the mothers of the victims of all these school shootings, and the mothers of those who did the shooting. For the mothers of the survivors, and the mothers who sat in front of their TVs in horror, hugging their child who just came home from school, safely.*

I deeply feel the pain of the former and the joy of the latter.

➤ *This is for young mothers stumbling through diaper changes and sleep deprivation.*

I say to them, "Hang in there. It goes fast, too fast. How lucky you are!"

➤ *And mature mothers learning to let go.*

I'm still struggling....

➤ *For working mothers and stay-at-home mothers. Single mothers and married mothers. Mothers with money, mothers without.*

And golfing mothers, like my Mom. And brave mother's like my Nana and Mama Sara.

.....And for you, my precious children. My wonderful adults. I like you, I love you and I miss you so much!

Love,
Momma

Mimosa Along the Old Trail

2000

Maggie, our golden retriever, hadn't been back to the old bike trail in six years. She was Jim's retirement gift from his company. We picked her out together and tied a little yellow string around her neck to mark her as ours amongst the pile of other puppies. She was only six and one half weeks and we'd come back to take her home when she was eight weeks.

The last person to take her to the trail might have been the dog walker when Jim was too sick to walk her. But Jim used to take her there three times a day, even after he was on the morphine and using a cane, crippled from the cancer eating his hipbone. I would be out for a while in my car and return to discover Jim sitting innocently in his blue living room chair like he'd been there for hours. But then he would mention something about how Maggie "didn't finish her business". That's when I knew he was driving under the influence of heavy morphine intoxication…all that was left to treat his illness…just something for the pain. He was always a bit of a fibber and he'd sneak his cigarettes when he told me he had stopped (how could you miss that?). So sneaking out to take Maggie and hold on to some semblance of routine was not surprising. Life was rapidly departing. Very rapidly. Just seventy-two days from diagnosis until our parting, though we didn't know the day or hour…. A story played out a million times a day. Just a different life or illness. But this was our life disappearing with oxygen tubes running up the stairs from a machine I don't remember renting. And Jim waking me up in the middle of the night saying we'd be late for Bill and Hillary's wedding (we personally didn't know the president). And me going insane because my husband was insane from the calcium breakdown in his bones poisoning his brain. They said he actually died of that: hyper-calcemia but the death certificate didn't mention the cancer that caused it.

One horrific time, just about two weeks before he went somewhere else, was when he began to undress in the living room in front of my daughter who was home for the weekend from college and him mumbling the whole time like one of those crazy street people. I called an ambulance after he tried to light a cigarette inside the trashcan. But that stink of a husband would act perfectly normal when his family was around and they'd say, "Isn't he doing great?" and "Boy, he looks terrific!" They thought I was exaggerating. I was in hell.

I was going rapidly mad and isolated from all sanity during this time. Just 72 days but it felt like 7200. It was, it had to be that long. Time slowed down and I stopped feeling anything for him. I later found out this was the way the spouse or caregiver survives. I would sit on the edge of the bed when he asked me to read from a book my sister loaned him entitled *The Psalms*. I would sit as far from him as I could and read aloud to him in a flat monotone. Those words might have comforted him but meant nothing to me. Read this and get it over with so I can pretend this isn't happening. Jim wasn't overtly religious. A catholic-gone-baptist one year prior. I didn't know what was going on when he switched. I was brought up Presbyterian but went to a baptist church because they didn't care I had been divorced from my first husband nor that I was generally weird.

One morning he sat on the edge of the bed in his underwear and it would seem he was being raised up, like he was trying to lift and go up, like "Is this how Jim will die? Sitting up and then 'poof' he's gone?" Then he took a small face towel with little lambs on it that I had given him in case he got sick. He very, very slowly and carefully folded it in half, long ways, held it carefully between his two hands together in front of him and brought it slowly to his forehead and then his lips. Was he having a little mass? What was happening? He was in his morphine stupor and totally somewhere else. I watched and wondered. Somebody said later he had been an alter boy in his youth. I think I knew that. He told me some of the naughty tricks he played on the priest and how he was always in trouble. He remembered it fondly.

It wasn't far to the trail by Bronco (Jim's car) but it was a hefty walk. I think he may have taken her once or twice on foot when he was hale and hearty. And Jim was, or appeared very hale, as he worked out in the gym at least three days a week and then fast walks every day...all since his early retirement just four years before he died from the devil's disease. He only smoked for thirty-five years. He tried patches. But this was his last addiction. He was a totally addicted alcoholic that, mercifully, did not have another drop of the stuff in ten years. Jim was magnificent, brave, true and reverent (not really) but totally memorable to all that knew him.

During the two visits of a Hospice nurse, Maggie would try to get between Jim and the visiting nurse to keep her from hurting him with the needle to draw blood. Her muzzle turned white when he died. No kidding, almost over night. Everybody that knew us commented on this. Jim and Maggie did not have one night apart except for our honeymoon.

Though I didn't know it was Jim's last day home, around noon I went to the corner hutch and took out the pewter chalice I had bought for our wedding toast. (We had special ordered non-alcoholic champagne for the toast and shared it in the chalice at the reception).

I then went to the fridge and poured some O'Doul's into the chalice. I held it out for Jim who was sitting in his blue chair and asked him, "Do you want a sip?" He took a sip and then so did I. Maggie and E.G. (our cat) were lying right at Jim's feet so I offered Maggie a sip and then E.G. Both of them lapped at it. Jim said it tasted really good savoring that one sip like he had been outside on a long hot summer day. And I knew the Mass he had started a few days before was continuing. Everything was spontaneous, sweet and peaceful. The rest of the work was Jim's to do. The dying part. He wouldn't let the paramedics put him on the stretcher so he walked out held up on each side. He did everything with integrity though I feel I failed miserably.

Once at Hospice for the next ten days, I couldn't bear to touch or hold him unless I immediately left the room to pace a thousand paces in that small but wonderful death house. He heard me say that it was okay for him to "Go". He'd been there about nine days by then. They say they need permission to go. Anyway, I think he heard me. He was already into a nether world, on his way somewhere. He just kept up that horrible breathing. The deep gasps that made each one seem like it would be the last. Oh God, I remember it all. But our bond was there in spite of my separation from it. Hard to explain. Bound to each other but I would keep on living. I wish I had been eighty so I could have gone with him. Harder when you are younger. My beautiful Jim who was 'just a kick in the pants'.

Maggie is now over ten years old. She's my last link to Jim in the most personal sense though his family and I remain in relatively frequent contact. Mag sleeps with me and will lay her head across my neck to get me up in the morning and pout when she doesn't go for a ride.

Last weekend we went back to the trail for the first time and she remembered it all. Walking back to the car, I pulled off a fuzzy mimosa blossom and breathed in its very sweet scent. And so did Maggie. It died in my hand.

Fifty

2001

Fifty! Impossible but here it comes, a big birthday. I find myself feeling every bit of my age. Things are dropping. Fat seems to roll down and forward now. Gravity is taking its toll, pulling everything toward the center of the earth. I'm surprised that feet don't get bigger during this process although my feet have become sore.

I'm feeling losses of every sort: physical, emotional, and menopausal. My daughter was giving me that look during a recent visit that says, "Boy, Mom you're looking older now."

Gee, I've made it to fifty! Isn't that a better approach to the thing? There have been no hard birthdays prior to this one. I'm trying to remember how Jim and I marked my fortieth. I think he called me an "old broad". But it was endearing. What would he call me *now*!?

My emotional heart is young and still knows how to beat a rapid love song and ache with each loss. But it probably is showing signs of clogging from the first twinkie at age five through last week's butter on toast. I read that we begin to clog our tubing at age three. So that's forty-seven years of build up. My good guy cholesterol is vectoring the right way however. I know how to eat well but seldom do it. I certainly know how to live well.

Every experience has added wisdom. Some things I stupidly don't get the first time so try them again and fail again. Repeating some things like the rings in a tree.

We *are* like trees. Our DNA isn't all that different, you know. The widening circles in the trunk don't just represent growth…they mark life and maturity. Each ring represents the food and water that was used during an age. And then it uses that 'stuff' until the next layer is created and so on: Some thin gaps, some wider depending on the weather, all a little uneven around the edges. Circles farther and farther from the core, the life-force, of the tree. I'm putting down new layers alright. Physical ones for sure, but too many ragged edged "maturing" ones for my liking.

I'm still weathering storms but not as well as I used to. I now need mostly sunny days and comfortable humidity…about seventy-two degrees is perfect. Yet I can't stop nature from bending, nearly breaking me. Testing my bark.

I'm doing fairly well, considering the stresses outside. But I'm not ready for the roots to go down too deep. Only in the last half-decade have little twig arms matured into branches. But I don't want to be the tree. I want to be a solitary leaf that experiences the newness and color of life, leaving only fodder for the grass.

Life is thrilling. I want to experience everything new and beautiful and interesting and soar aloft sucking in and using every nutrient that is given by grace.

On my birthday I will have completed fifty years. Only five decades. The next ones will require the maturity I haven't yet found.

If I really was a leaf, I bet I'd be a nice pretty yellow now, not yet turning to bright orange, floating by and smiling to all the other nice leaves as they float by….

One More Friend, Thus this Book

2001

This long-distance friend is the first person I trusted to read certain xcerpts that might be included in a book. He is way too direct and honest – an nathema to my Pollyanna upbringing. How delightful. I knew I could expect ie truth from him…and I got it.   This curmudgeon not only said nice things bout the pieces, but in one surprising moment he made me realize that telling iy story could, might, perhaps, possibly, make a difference.

The first journal-story was bravely attached to an email I sent him after e retired. The story was about the ice in Rosslyn. He of course recognized the ile, told me how inaccurate it was (which it was in certain spots) and agreed it ould be used in a book, if I would just get the facts right! (Thankfully, he pproved what is in this book). While he still slings the occasional barb at me, m amazed that I can now laugh at the truth. What a glorious thing.

And so he has taught me. What did he do, you ask, that made me think iy storytelling might be helpful to people in some way?   This same man that ft me behind slogging through ice and frozen slush, recently walked by my ide to dinner. His hands were shoved down in his pockets and yet, with a little runt and elbow put out at the slightest angle, he offered me that small open iace to hold on.

Role in My Life: He was the final inspiration to publish the book. He *'as well known as a heartless curmudgeon but after reading some of my stories,* *e began to notice the path in front of us, offer his arm or an alternative route* *nd blessed my soul. Although he still thinks some of my writings are* *vhining".*

The Huge Slice of "Ritch" Chocolate Cake
Brewski's, Hermosa Beach

PostScript

September 2001

I arrived in Los Angeles from Washington Dulles less than twenty-four hours before the conflagration in New York, Pennsylvania and Washington. Five of my colleagues had changed their flight or cancelled their attendance at a meeting scheduled for September 11, 2001. It was a miracle or luck or fate or whatever you believe, but they were not aboard their usual flight, American Airlines #77. Those who lost their lives that morning from the air or on the ground are now spared the fear and reality we are experiencing.

I was numb and unable to focus while grounded in LA, like so many around the world. The book and finishing it certainly seemed trivial. When I finally returned home relevancy came to me.

Our world is broken. I am broken. But with every imperfection in this world there are nuggets, ritch lodes of strength, abiding love, beauty and hope that nothing can destroy. We are fearful, yet oddly strengthened and unified against it. We are anxious but help each other and dispel our anxiety.

I expect to feel shame when the book is published, but it is a very familiar feeling. Perhaps my shame will redeem one reader's shame. If you are poor, wealthy, African, African-American, Asian, Hispanic, deaf, fat, blind, bald, skinny, short, Islam, Jew, Christian, young, old, tall, mean, nice, gorgeous, gay, crippled, Texan, Canadian, Russian, Australian, cat, dog, martian or maniacal fanatic you know what it is to be hurt, mocked, loathed, rejected, even hated. No one is exempt. Writing this book has taken away the power of my shame, the pain and the anger while destroying my façade, my ego and denial of my imperfection. There it is for all to see. It is my truth.

I hope you will treasure the precious, ritch and wonderful moments that surround you without focusing on the blight in the world or in yourself. Celebrate the differences even though it's hard and never give up hope on the love that is the Kernel of our hearts.

And dance in the bosom of acceptance...